# THE MASK JEWS WEAR

The Self-Deceptions of American Jewry

D1017732

OTHER BOOKS BY THE AUTHOR

*A Layman's Introduction to Religious Existentialism*
*A New Jewish Theology in the Making*
*How Can a Jew Speak of Faith Today?*
*Choosing a Sex Ethic*

# THE MASK JEWS WEAR

The Self-Deceptions of American Jewry

by EUGENE B. BOROWITZ

SH'MA
A JOURNAL OF JEWISH RESPONSIBILITY
PORT WASHINGTON, N.Y.

ISBN 0-671-21549-3
Library of Congress Catalog Card Number: 73-7926
Designed by Irving Perkins
Manufactured in the United States of America

Paperback edition
Type set and printed by
The Tabard Press Corp
New York, N.Y. 10014

*To Steven S. Schwarzschild*

# Contents

# CHAPTER 1

# An Invitation to Self-Examination

For about twenty-five years now, I have been talking to Jews about being Jewish. As a theologian, I would prefer to talk to them about Judaism, the nature of its faith, the tone of its practice. But what most Jews are interested in is the fact of their Jewishness. Just what does being a Jew mean? And why should it matter to anyone? Some say they rather like being Jewish, but cannot see why they should be expected to work at it. They don't mind sending their children for a Jewish education, but they also warn them not to take it too seriously. Others, having the best of Western culture available to them, do not see that what the Jewish community and its traditions offer is worth the bother. And still others are so negative they now refuse to discuss the topic altogether.

Until recently, I took these encounters at face value. I believed people who said that their Jewishness was marginal to their existence, that—to use the common expression—they really weren't very Jewish. I no longer am so easily convinced. The substance of the argument has not shifted. Jews still say they do not care much about being Jewish, and it remains clear that on the manifest level, in terms of what they know and do and say, there is little in them that one could call Jewish. Still, in our changed social situation, listening to them now in existential depth, I hear something different. Statements that I once took to reflect an authentic sense of self now regularly strike me as formulas of self-deception. We are not, I think, who we say we are. The truth about us, I have come to think, is that we are more fundamentally Jewish than we are willing to admit.

I now see most American Jews as a new species of Marrano. In Spain during the fourteenth and fifteenth centuries, Jews had to convert to Catholicism to survive. But while they affected a Catholic exterior, they remained steadfastly Jewish at heart. In the United States freedom, not intimidation, has created an inverse form of crypto-Jewishness. We say to anyone who asks, "We're really not very Jewish." Perhaps in recent years we've become more concerned about our Jewishness—the children, Auschwitz, the State of Israel and all that sort of thing—but, taking our surface selves as our true identity, we believe our Jewishness does not go very deep. The old Marranos were another breed. Because Catholicism was forced upon them, they did not confuse their real identity with what society insisted that they be on the surface. But we willingly, avidly turned from the outer signs of our Jewishness to embrace the style of American liberalism. We have been such eager converts to our urban, educated way of life that it comes as a shock to us to discover in an odd moment how Jewish we still are. We are Marranos in reverse, for we have repressed our inner identity. The time has come to end this inauthenticity and learn again to say without hyphenation or other qualification: We are Jews.

I recognize that all this is quite an assertion, and I propose to spend the rest of this book clarifying it.

My judgment in this matter results from the use of a somewhat uncommon methodology and is an inference from a choice that contemporary society is forcing upon us.

I shall be analyzing the question of Jewishness in existential terms. Despite some years of popularity for Martin Buber and Franz Rosenzweig, existential analysis remains a relatively unfamiliar procedure. (Indeed, one acquainted with Buber and Rozenzweig will not find much here that he can directly associate with them, for I employ their approach to Jewishness in a way that they did not utilize.) The oldest and most common method of discussing being Jewish is in terms of observance of the commandments. With the rise of a modern Jewry, whose overwhelming majority was not fully observant, that gave way to Jewishness as loyalty to an idea: ethical monotheism. And, when that turned out to be too rationalistic to incorporate the riches of actual Jewish existence, we tried to think of ourselves as a folk or a nationality, somehow linked up with the notion of ethical monotheism. By any of those standards our Jewishness does not go very deep.

I think that does not tell us the whole truth, because Jewishness, to me, is best understood today as a certain set of self, a particular existential stance. It is a way of basing one's life on one's relation to the Jewish people, its tradition and its values, especially its faith. I am not saying that observance and ideas and folk have nothing to do with being Jewish. I rather feel that Jewishness begins with the self and that, once this Jewishness is acknowledged and made the effective basis of our lives, it results in a life style easily identifiable as Jewish. Thus, the purpose of my writing is not purely intellectual. For, while I would like people to understand their existential Jewishness, I am hoping that insight will move them to live out their Jewishness.

But I am getting ahead of myself. I want to clarify my frame of reference for you, since it is somewhat unfamiliar, yet I do not think it will be useful to say very much about it abstractly.

You will understand it best as we apply it. Nonetheless, since you must be quite an active partner in this procedure, it is important that you have some idea of what we shall be doing.

The various existentialist approaches are concerned less with the mind and its structures than with the self and its freedom. To know man means to know his full personhood and not merely his intellect. They deny that he has within him an unchanging essence, a permanent substance as simple as it is immaterial, which medieval thinkers called a *soul*. If he did, our task would be to define what constitutes a Jewish, as distinct from a general human, soul. Bizarre though such a thought may seem to modern men, it seems implicit in the thought of Yehudah Halevi (1075–1141) and is an explicit basis of the teaching of Shneour Zalman of Lyady (1747–1813) carried on today by the popular Lubavitch Hasidim.

For the existentialist the self must be understood in far more dynamic terms. A man is less something given or arrived at, than something continually in process of becoming. If there is such a thing as an essence to man it is, so to speak, his freedom to choose what he will be. Naturally there are always many limits to what we might do, but it is just in our response to the alternatives available that we exercise our humanity. Thus, we may get a good sense of who we are by focusing on those moments when we must make some basic choice of how we shall live. Heidegger has pointed to our attitude toward our death as critical, and Jaspers has more broadly spoken of "limit situations." In keeping with the times in which we live, I shall be concentrating on our choice of values. I shall move from the choice to what it tells us of the person, from the value affirmed to what it implies about the self in which it takes its ground.

The open and dynamic element in human character is usually stabilized in most people by commitment to certain basic values which one holds on to, with modification, as life proceeds. This fundamental personal stance is normally a combination of various concerns. In the usual course of things they hold together nicely. In times of personal or social stress, the old balance of values can no longer be maintained. We must choose which we care about more—in Abraham's classic dilemma, obedience to God or love of Isaac. In such a crisis, as we give up one value to affirm another, we determine who, in fact, we now are. That is, I take it, the basis of the extraordinary appeal of existentialist literary heroes from Dostoyevsky's Raskolnikov to Bellow's Artur Sammler.

We Americans are in such a moment of trial now. Our urban, educated, upper-middle class finds central elements in its basic life style in increasing disharmony. Something in our previous aggregation of values must now be given second place. Watching American Jews make this choice, I think we can gain a new sense of what their Jewishness is and what it means to them.

Let me drop back in time to a somewhat more stable situation —say, to the 1950's or early 1960's. There was then what sweepingly but not unreasonably may be called a liberal style. Politically that included the intellectuals of the Democratic party and a spectrum embracing meliorative socialists on the left and change-oriented Republicans on the right. Their ideas came from *The New Republic* or *The Nation,* more militantly from *I. F. Stone's Weekly* or more discreetly from preachments in *The Saturday Review.* They wanted the federal government to make America more fully democratic and the United Nations to pacify the world. Their confidence in man, education and creativity carried over into culture. At the symphony they called for more contemporary music. In their homes they chose furnishings of modern design and accents of folk craft. In their schools they promoted progressive education. In their communities they were the reliable audience for theater, lecture and recital series. I remember them well, having been one of their number.

What strikes me as I think about those days is the relatively seamless quality of that life. It all fit together so well. I am thinking specifically of three of its elements which today stand in conflict: our idealism, our realism and our hedonism. Then it seemed

quite clear that we would fulfill ourselves by bettering our society. World War II made sense, and so did the long self-denial
of advanced education or working for a decent place in the capi-
talist system. Realism meant that change came through politics
and applied intelligence. So, for most Jews the liberal style now
took the place that Jewishness had held in their parents' lives.
With it there came a new attention to pleasure, to cuisine and
furnishings, to recreation and travel. For a decade or more, as
the economy expanded and with it social freedom, the liberal
way seemed to have proved itself.

How long ago that seems now. Not that the style is dead or
forgotten. It lives among us in many useful ways. But its spirit is
broken. Worse, it seems almost impossible to restore coherence
among its divergent strands.

On the first level this is largely because of our hard-won, deepened sense of realism bought at the price of the assassination of
two Kennedys and a King, of the credibility of Presidents Johnson and Nixon, of the frustration at being unable to end a war
almost everyone recognized was undesirable, of the pain that
our economy when bad demeans us and when good dehumanizes
us, of the daily guilt at the poor we do not feed, the ethnic rival-
ries we cannot tame, the racial hatreds we cannot overcome. We
men, it turns out, are not very smart and certainly not very
moral. The best of five-year plans do not change things very
much. Self-interest, we learn with every television news show, is
the fundamental rule of human nature. A wise man pays close
attention to where the power is and, even more, to how it is
structured through classes and institutions. We have learned all
this, but we have suffered from the education. Perhaps if we had
not hoped so much and personally tried so hard (comparatively
speaking), we would not now suffer so much disillusion. But it
is this tougher sense of what is realistic that characterizes post-
liberal man.

This new realism has upset the old balance between idealism
and hedonism. Pleasure has a higher priority in our lives today,

and not only because we are more affluent than we once were. The truth is, we do not trust the world or our society or the people around us very much. We are far more likely to get aggravation rather than satisfaction from them. So we are not much inclined to sacrifice our enjoyment for the common need, the delight of the moment for the larger hope of the future. We prefer to play now and pay later. We wish to be experts in what to eat and where to go or whatever other delights, from meditation to orgasm, will gratify us. Why not? In this crazy world, who knows what tomorrow will bring?

By contrast, idealism seems naïve. What realistic reason can one give for living to a high ethical standard or trying to build a society reflecting justice and compassion? Realism not only means the demythologizing of the traditional sources of morality —religion, society, education, reason—but demythologizing man himself. He may be the only source of value in what Camus, in a moment of optimism, called a benignly indifferent universe, but he is nasty, brutish and unstable. Indeed, if we are to face him as he is, then we must come to the continuing trauma of our time, his persistent desire to be violent. We are just beginning to realize how vicious even ordinary men can be. So, if fulfillment is our greatest good, then why not a measure of violence? Clint Eastwood can be our cowboy hero and Sam Peckinpah our idea of creative talent.

The end of the old liberal synthesis is symbolized in the situation of two of our major intellectual journals today. The *New York Review of Books* began liberal but quickly moved on to radicalism; and *Commentary,* which had for some years been near the anti-Communist left, shifted to the political center or, some insist, to the conservative right. Neither could face the 1970's with the attitudes that suited an older, less troubled time.

Our American dilemma is that we do not wish to give up our old idealism while we practice a new hedonism in the name of a deeper realism. We would like to keep them together in something of the harmony they knew a few years ago. But our realism has shown life to be so a-ethical that it is difficult for us to say why we should undertake its burdens, which, realistically, we know will be great. Day by day, the revelations of the venality and stupidity around us urge us to reorder our priorities and make self-gratification the major good of our lives. Instead of a little pleasure now and then to make life bearable, why not make the pursuit of pleasure our major goal? As the title of a recent book on the Fitzgerald era put it, "Living well is the best revenge."

This challenge, made possible by affluence, made visible by advertising, made attractive by the beautiful people, comes with special force to the Jew. Being disproportionately urban, educated and secularized, having chosen the liberal way of life as a substitute for his parents' Jewishness, the Jew now finds his fundamental life style thrown into question. And it is in response to this American value crisis that the Jew, like others, will determine who, in reality, he is.

The ground upon which this entire book stands is my observation that many Jews, despite the new realism, insist on giving ethics a high personal priority. They may not know quite how one should act amid our complex problems—only the radicals have self-confidence as well as idealism—but they know that there is no life worthy of the name without strong moral effort. After centuries of Jewish deprivation they intend to have such pleasure as they can. But they know that for them indulgence cannot be the meaning of existence.

Not all Jews today make that choice. A good many have as good as gone the way of hedonism—a dubious recompense for having been freed of the yoke of the Torah. Others have not yet, or have only barely, become conscious of the question. What interests me is how, over the past few years, some Jews have with increasing consciousness seen the need to make a choice of values and have insisted that, for them, the humane values remain primary. Those Jews, and others in vague ways moving with them, are the people I wish to address here. I want to explore with them what this choice of values says about their identity. I want to help them investigate what sort of existential stance is behind their idealism despite their realism. And I hope to show that, for many of us, it is our Jewishness that has, perhaps with a power we had not believed it still had over us, reasserted itself. I shall return to all these matters later. For now let us spend a few moments clarifying the approach we shall be taking.

Most of the time I shall be working in terms of three levels of analysis: the intellectual, the psychological and the existential. At our human best such distinctions are artificial. So when we are confronted with the need to act, we can often knit our raveled selves together and, for good or ill, do something as whole persons. And our inability to act, these days, often springs from the impossibility of bringing mind and heart and self together enough to choose one course of action over another. Yet it is just the situation of modern man, the glory and the curse of contemporary self-consciousness, that reason and emotion and selfhood have been segregated from each other and educated to live in belligerent coexistence. So we must keep these distinctions in mind as we proceed—but with the conscious purpose of moving through ideas and feelings to their ground in the self. Let me clarify that somewhat.

Mostly, when men talk about themselves, they give voice to the philosophy they have worked out over the years to explain why they have lived their lives as they have. It is always difficult to know how much confidence to place in such ideas about oneself. Wise men have always trusted talk less than action; cynics have always considered it a cover for self-interest. In our time the issue of personal credibility has grown increasingly complex. Freud taught us that most ideas are a rationalization of our unconscious needs and fantasies. Marx taught us that they serve class interests. And as we were digesting these lessons, Sartre and

Camus pointed out that in extreme situations—as under the Nazis —it was impossible to tell from what men had said what, in fact, they would do.

A similar shock ran through American campuses in recent years when, during the various upheavals, students and alumni discovered the distance between what professors had taught as desirable and what they themselves did in a crisis. In such a world, ideas are still a useful currency, but we cannot put our ultimate trust in them. We must listen with respect when people intellectualize about themselves, for they know their topic better than anyone else. Still, we listen critically, and instead of limiting our interest to their thoughts, we would like to know just what, in human terms, they mean by them.

In our discussion, then, we shall be interested in ideas about Jewishness but cannot be satisfied with them. We shall want to go beyond what people say being Jewish means to them, to the personal realities that lie behind their thoughts.

To get to know someone these days means to pay as much attention to his emotions as to his ideas, if not more. Experience and the psychologists have taught us that people are far more likely to act in terms of their childhood fantasies and youthful associations than in terms of their philosophy. We see that most clearly when they undertake a role such as teacher, parent or rabbi. Now they are expected to say certain things—for example, that they love children, believe in experimentation and want to be flexible. We will worry about their competence if we do not hear them utilize some of the concepts we associate with the role. But a listener does not have to give a Rorschach test or conduct a psychoanalytic interview to be aware that there are varying emotional realities behind these phrases. Some possibilities move and arouse the person. Others are firmly shut off or are expressed only with resentment. One quickly learns to listen to professional people less in terms of what they say than in terms of what excites them. They may know all about what someone in their role should do, but one may count on their doing effectively only that which touches their emotions.

The same is true in our personal life. Largely it is our emotions that determine what we will do. My favorite current example—perhaps because it is so dramatic—is of a young Maoist friend. I came to know him in his Jewish period, when his devotion and piety were quite extraordinary for one brought up in a family estranged from Judaism in the usual middle-class way. However, his personal problems were sufficiently great that, despite his Jewish spiritual satisfactions, he undertook psychoanalytic treatment. He came to realize that he had espoused Judaism so seriously only as a morally acceptable means of unconsciously killing off his father, while creating in God the good father he felt he had never had.

Some years of psychiatry liberated him from "all that" and, he felt, from the need of further treatment. He then became a devout Maoist, to the extent that one of his most recent attempts to create a modern theater was a drama showing how a Chinese village was converted to Communism. In his case, though the intellectual verbiage has changed, the emotional realities have remained the same. Only, now the bad father is Western imperialism and the good father, Chairman Mao. His theories about world history and the good society are not thereby invalidated, but I cannot dissociate them, in his case, from his inner psychological dynamics. His thought says more about his personal structure than about mankind's situation, and I only wish he had stayed with his doctor somewhat longer or had had a more perceptive analyst.

The same need to reach for our emotional depths is true of our coming to understand what being Jewish means to us. I do not see how one can realistically talk about Jewishness without confronting his individual mixture of love and hate for it. To be a Jew is almost never an unemotional thing. Our emotional investment in it is sometimes evident only in the extensive retraining we have undertaken so as not to react to the inner promptings of community upbringing and social conditioning. Nonetheless, repressed though they may be, the feelings move us.

With all that, I think we must pursue our analysis to an even deeper level. We need to probe beyond conscious feelings and unconscious dynamisms to what I have been calling, in existentialist fashion, the basic stance of the self. I think we can make clear why that is related to the emotional realm yet differs from it, if we focus for a moment on the problem of values. Normally we can tell what a person truly cares about by noting the emotional freight it carries in his life, what the psychiatrists call *affect*. So, to go back to our examples of people in roles, the teacher, parent or rabbi who gets animated talking about some tutoring his child did or turns slightly acid because his student became interested in a rival school of interpretation, tells us a good deal about his values. Because feelings are relatively accessible, we have come to equate feelings about things with having values toward them. Thus, we tend to reduce understanding someone to understanding his emotions.

I am suggesting that, while there is a good deal of overlapping between affect and value, analytically, the values are prior—only secondarily do we charge them with emotion. (I would, however, agree that most of our intermediate and specific values are the result more of emotional growth and rational choice than of our most fundamental way of confronting reality.)

This distinction in the levels of selfhood shows up quite clearly as a modern psychiatric problem: the patient who has no desire to get well. He does not care about self-fulfillment, abundant living or some other accepted goal of living. One may say that this itself is a sign of sickness, but that is hardly a self-evident truth. There are philosophies in the East that consider the self a delusion and adjustment to the reality of the world around us as the root folly of normal human existence. Thus, what constitutes emotional health or sickness is itself dependent upon one's prior sense of value. The sort of health one should strive for is determined not solely by a psychological judgment but more by what one believes being alive is or ought to be. There is a sense, then, in which one must truly care in a certain way before one can hope to get better. Our psychiatry, therefore, depends upon a commitment to a certain sense of life. It can work only if the patient, like the doctor, already values a self-affirming, world-accepting style and, for the sake of better achieving it, is willing to undertake the arduous discipline of psychiatric analysis.

This elemental level of the self, connected to, yet lying beyond, mind and heart, is what I should like to talk about and reach. Understanding Jewishness as ideas and sentiments will inevitably be shallow, in my opinion, unless we connect it with that deepest sense of what it means to be a person.

Gaining access to such depths in ourselves is not easy. Even on the first two levels most people try to avoid thinking about their lives with any degree of rigor, and breaking through the defenses we erect against psychological insight is a major part of the psychiatric healing process. Yet philosophy is an old and honored activity and, in recent decades, Freud's teaching has been considered an invaluable therapy for the emotionally ill. By contrast, the existentialist analysis of what it means to be human is still coming into its own, having been established more as a literary than as an intellectual movement until our own time. Now that we utilize its lenses we can see how geniuses of an earlier time—Jeremiah, Job, Yehudah Halevi and the Baal Shem Tov quickly come to mind—penetrated behind cognition and passion to some central point of their existence. They were rare even among the great teachers of our past, so we have few models by which to shape our existentialist search. Yet we have come to learn enough of what it means to be a self that we have some notion of how we must proceed.

The most basic principle is that this is a process no one can do for someone else. I may try to be of help to you in breaking through to your basic sense of identity, but I cannot tell you who you really are. I have some ideas that I think are true about many, perhaps most, Jews. But each person is unique. You may not be one of the group I understand, or you may be so in a way all your own. Whatever the case, you must search the matter out for yourself; and only you can ultimately know whether the conclusions you reach are as true to you as they might be or whether, for reasons of your own, you have ended the search at some other point.

An investigation whose focus is so personal would best be carried out face to face. A book is a poor substitute for the situation in which two people confront each other honestly and come to know, through agreement and dissent, what each truly cares about. But putting these words on paper, as impersonal as that may have to be, is my way of sharing with more than a few people what my experience in many such encounters has taught me.

I suggest that you follow a certain path with me. First we will give the historical setting of our situation. This procedure, incidentally, will lay bare some of the major psychological mechanisms society has created in us. Then we shall turn to some forms of rejecting our Jewishness, those which assert that we do not need it to lead the good life. This encounter will then lead us to the positive assessments that, with increasing comprehensiveness, describe the scope of what it means to be truly a Jew. I deal with the negative reactions first, because, as long as they have not been overcome, it will do no good to try to make positive assertions about our Jewishness. They will be canceled out by our unspoken rejection of things Jewish.

My first approach to all our statements about our Jewishness is to be concerned with what is true in them. None of the suggestions considered here is anywhere near totally false. Rather, as I see it, each has seized an aspect of the multifaceted Jewish self and raised it to a theory of the whole. We should not lose the partial truth when we reject the theory as not satisfactory in its entirety. So we shall try to separate the valid claim from that which overstates it and then, with greater difficulty, seek a way of integrating it with the other claims about Jewishness so that they make a reasonably coherent whole. Our procedure in moving from the historical backgrounds of our situation to negative responses to Jewishness and then on to positive theories of its meaning should prove useful in attaining a comprehensive view, because it is essentially cumulative.

The second part of the analysis, however, is polemic. My concern here is to help you see how, for all its merits, most theses are inadequate to express a proper sense of Jewishness. I shall not forget my notion that our quest here is primarily a self-examination on the part of the reader, with me acting as his guide. As a result, I shall not attempt to demonstrate the reader's intellectual inadequacy by adducing masses of data, numerous literary references or other such signs of authority. Such displays of power—particularly by the professionally trained—only silence the reader. They rarely lead to insight. Instead, I shall try by example and analysis to help the reader see the ways in which a given proposal does not square with values that I assume he holds. Hence I shall try to show that he needs a theory of self more adequate to his values. Since, as I propose to show, for many of us our Jewishness is related to our values, we need a more adequate theory of Jewishness to explain the commitments of our Jewish selves. So, the process is one of seeking out one's values, of seeing their relation to being Jewish and, finally, of trying to understand how self and values and Jewishness all fit together.

Some people would call that an inverted or backward argument. Logically one should establish one's principles and from this derive one's values. But we are in a living situation. We are not starting our inquiry into Jewishness as if, like some devotee of Descartes, we could jump out of history and begin with pure mind engaging in pure doubt. Instead, we shall proceed from some few values that, even in this time of crisis, we are tolerably sure of. We know that we care about these and, in the face of the freedom to choose other values, know that it is the humane ones on which we stake our lives. So I am suggesting that we reason from our values to their ground, from what we care about to what we are, from that about which we are reasonably sure to that which we may therefore come to know and affirm.

Each person, of course, needs to discover himself. He alone can estimate what he is committed to; he alone can judge what is its ground. As we move from theory to theory, you should come to know better what you really stand for and why. If it turns out that you do not have the ethical-cultural commitment basic to the secularized Jewish life style, we shall have little basis upon which to proceed. Or, equally important, you may discover that you do not feel that your values have the depth or grounding that I discern behind this way of facing life. In that case, for you my analysis is wrong. In any case, since most of us are not sensitive to, and do not deliberately hide from, an awareness of the existential depth in which our values arise, I shall concentrate my efforts on trying to help you reach it.

Since who you are is so personal a matter, I would refute myself and my understanding of what we are about if I proceeded directly and substantively rather than indirectly and evocatively. Mostly I shall proceed by a species of intellectual provocation. I often will not accept as true or adequate a statement about Jewishness that many people consider self-evident or indisputable. Too often I find such acceptance an excuse for not confronting who we are. What seems conventional Jewish wisdom is often a defense against self-search. By not taking such things for granted, by asking a further question when polite people normally stop, by bringing in an example that is disturbing because it breaks the stereotype of Jewish question and official response, I hope to find a way to move you to respond from your depths. I am sorry if that also irritates you. I would prefer not to annoy you, but that is the emotional side effect of having the old integration of one's self challenged.

Since I think that that old sense of self keeps us from the truth we seek, delving below the stereotyped response is critical to our inquiry. I shall try to limit my provocation to what is useful. In reacting to my probing, I suggest that you ask yourself again and again not merely What do I think and how do I feel? but What sorts of things have I been able and unable to get myself to do as a Jew? What are the real decisions I have made about my values and my Jewishness, and to what questions have I refused to give an answer? It may turn out that you are that rare person whose choices have closely paralleled what you have said to yourself about yourself. For most of us, I think, the subtle contrasts or open conflicts between actual existence and self-image reveal a rather significant split of self. And that is where you can learn for yourself, through yourself, what your real sense of Jewishness is.

Since I cannot know which idea or combination of ideas a given reader may hold, I have tried to work with all those that I keep coming across in the Jewish community. Not only do these vary from person to person, but there are even regional differences. In Ohio, where I grew up, it was and remains most natural to think of Jews as being part of a "religion" somewhat in the way Protestants and Catholics think of themselves. In the New York suburb where I have lived for some years now, the sense of Jewish ethnicity is far more prevalent—and that was so long before the current explosion of Jewish ethnic sentiment. I find New England Jews typically responsive to calls to tradition, while Californians seem to get excited only about the possibility of creating the forms of tomorrow's Jewishness today. There is indeed a multiplicity of Jewish self-perceptions to consider. Yet I think one might well find the full range of attitudes that we will analyze here in any sizable Jewish community—and sometimes, I think, they are all present in every individual Jew, one way or another. If, as you read along, some of them turn out to be quite peripheral to your situation, I hope you will find them informative of what others in this variegated Jewish people think and what might perhaps be an option for you.

We begin now with a look at history.

# CHAPTER 2

# The Rise of the Modern Marrano

The split in the Jewish self is comparatively recent in the long record of Jewish history. The men of the Bible and the rabbis of Talmudic times asked why they were called to be prophets or why they had to suffer. They never demanded to know why they were Jews. Despite the persecutions of the Middle Ages, the normal Jewish question was not Why are we Jewish? but When will the Messiah come to save and redeem us? The new question arises only with a radically new social situation.

The old segregated pattern of Jewish existence in dispersion from the Land of Israel is justly symbolized by the ghetto. In its standard form, the Jewish residential quarter of a city was walled in and its gates were locked each sundown. Such ghettos came into being around the year 1500 and lasted only some three hundred years, before the advent of the Emancipation destroyed them. Many scholars think that the imposition of the ghetto may be traced back to the Jewish practice of living together in close community for protection from the Gentile and for companionship in maintaining the Jewish way of life. Thus, the *shtetl* of Eastern Europe was not created by an imposed physical barrier and the *mellahs* of North Africa were often unwalled. Nonetheless, these Jews too lived in isolated and relatively self-contained communities. So the image of the locked and guarded ghetto gates of Western Europe poignantly expresses the situation of the Jew for the fifteen centuries, from the year 300 (about when Christianity became the official religion of the Roman Empire) to 1800 (the time of the Emancipation). The ghetto sums up an era of legislated disabilities among Moslems and Christians alike: the businesses Jews might not enter, the social activities they might not engage in, the hats or badges or other distinguishing marks of Jewishness they had to wear, the conversionist sermons they had to listen to, the riots and pogroms to which they were subjected.

When we read of the conditions under which Jews lived during this extended medieval period, they strike us as extraordinarily trying and disturbing. That makes it all the more surprising that, as far as we can tell, throughout this period the typical Jew lived with great integrity of self. In Babylonia, Franco-Germany or Poland, during the Moslem conquests, the Crusades or the Cossack pogroms, the Jew knew who he was. He felt no conflict or ambiguity about his identity. His society had a definite place for him as a Jew, negative though it was, and he had a countervailing inner certainty of commitment which gave his Jewishness great worth and deep significance. The degraded status caused its own special problems; but, being firmly fixed and publicly accepted, it obviated all questions concerning identity.

As feudalism waned and cities rose to dominance, their commercial realities made a place for the energetic, capable Jew, and he came to be tolerated for his usefulness long before he was admitted as a citizen. Thus, in the millennium and a half of the Middle Ages, as the Jew stepped out of "the ghetto" each morning, he knew immediately where he stood in the world at large.

The continual denigration from without did not destroy him as a person, for he set the balance straight within: he was one of God's own people, chosen by Him for a separate existence and dispersed by Him among the nations; God loved him and his people. So, Jews possessed an inalienable dignity. Through those long centuries, as their Moslem and Christian rulers more intensively segregated and oppressed them, the Jews were not overwhelmed. To a surprising extent, they transcended the harsh cruelty of their social situation and lived with high human nobility. If anything, the venom of their defamers made evident for them the truth that they, not their persecutors, were being true to the image of God in man.

With the emancipation of the Jews, beginning about the time of the French Revolution, the lengthy medieval era of the Jews comes to an end. Imposed segregation ceased and careers were opened to talents—to use the symbol once again, the ghetto walls came down. The Jew was admitted into society as an equal and given full rights as a citizen. That, in theory was what the Emancipation meant.

Let me quickly state some qualifications. The Emancipation was not one dramatic event, but a long process, proceeding at best by fits and starts and with great regional variation. The United States, with little tradition to defend, gave the Jews freedom almost from the start. England, France, the German states, the Austro-Hungarian Empire, were much more liberal than the principalities and nations of Eastern Europe. There the Emancipation was tediously slow, to the extent, as some have argued, that it hardly took place at all. And in North Africa, it was only where the French took over at the beginning of the twentieth century that there was any equality for the Jews. In more backward Moslem countries there was none. Moreover, one can hardly say the emancipatory process has ever, anywhere, been completed. The dream of freedom and equality lives and in many places is somewhat realized, but many Jews in the freest of countries still find themselves facing social walls and psychic gates. And some countries, notably Russia, are less free than before.

The revolution in the social status of Jews has ended their degradation, but ironically has also destroyed their sure sense of self. The form of the problem is set by the social reconstruction that promised the Jew a full and equal role in society. After the disastrous Catholic-Protestant religious wars, the question of belief was increasingly sundered from the political realm and assigned to the area of private activity. The European state began to think of itself less as a Christian entity than as a secular one, neutral to the private religion of its citizens and tolerant of all faiths. That is why Jews could properly participate in it. The Jews in feudal times had necessarily been outsiders, for they could not swear the Christian oaths which tied one level of society to another. In the modern world the only interest the state, as such, came to have in one's Jewishness was whether it prevented or encouraged his being a good and loyal citizen. When Napoleon, in full imperial grandeur, summoned a Sanhedrin to speak for the French Jewish community, what he wanted from them was assurance that Jewish religious faith, privately held, did not interfere with civic responsibility as publicly enacted. Three of Napoleon's dozen questions placed the issue squarely before the Jewish notables: "No. 4. In the eyes of Jews, are Frenchmen not of the Jewish religion considered as brothers or as strangers? No. 5. What conduct does Jewish law prescribe toward Frenchmen not of the Jewish religion? No. 6. Do the Jews born in France and treated by the law as French citizens acknowledge France as their country? Are they bound to defend it? Are they bound to obey the laws and follow the directions of the civil code?" The Sanhedrin had little difficulty (except for the issue of intermarriage) in giving Napoleon what he wanted. They said, in effect, that Judaism, like Protestantism or Catholicism, is a spur to good citizenship and being Jewish is only, like Christianity, another way of being personally religious. Judaism becomes, so to speak, another church of Western man. As Christianity is welcome in the modern state as an expression of conscience, so Judaism could be welcome.

But this transformation of the Jewish position in society was also the beginning of the divided Jewish self. In the modern state, rights are given to individuals, not to groups. In the medieval world, Moslem or Christian, the Jews had a fixed place in society *as a community*. The individual Jew received his status only by virtue of being a member of the local Jewish community. If it did not acknowledge him, the larger community could treat him as an outlaw. So, Jewish communities until modern times were often quite zealous about who could immigrate into their midst or take up residence among them. Thus, too, the threat of excommunication from the recognized community was quite serious.

There was no question in the mind of those French rationalists who fought for Jewish rights in post-Revolutionary France that the rights were given on a personal not a communal basis. In the National Assembly's great debate on this topic in December, 1789, Mirabeau denounced the idea that Jews or anyone else could be a nation within the French nation. But it was Clermont Tonnere, their other great defender, who put the thesis in classic form: "To the Jews as a nation we must deny everything. To the Jews as individuals we must grant everything." In the secular state, the Jew no longer had to be a member of the Jewish community in order to have a place in things. That was given one by virtue of his being a citizen. One had the right to be a Jew, of course, but that was a private matter, an additional commitment, something one added on to what society now recognized as one's essential identity. In actual practice, day by day, one learned that there were large and significant areas of existence where one's Jewishness was completely irrelevant. Society now taught the Jew that he was basically a citizen who might, in other areas of his life, be a Jew. The freedom granted was extraordinary by previous Jewish experience. Yet the conditions under which it was given created a split in the Jewish soul. Its two parts became increasingly distant due to the attractiveness of the general society and the handicaps involved in remaining Jewish, even privately.

The medieval Jew knew society was hostile. The modern Jew has been emancipated, and in that act of emancipation he has seen an act of hospitality. He could not now easily justify his Jewishness on the grounds of the Gentiles' inhumanity. Rather the Jew took advantage of the opportunities offered by the Emancipation; as he wore the society's clothes, spoke its language, attended its schools, mastered its culture, benefited from its economy, he could not help but be impressed. Most Jews found that the *goyim* were not so bad, that the best of the new world extended and fulfilled their old Jewish hopes. People were encouraged to work and study and build a better world. Everyone seemed concerned to live in health and prosperity.

There were certainly problems and change was coming too slowly; but, by contrast to the ghetto, the richness of life offered by society was irresistible by personal and many Jewish standards. Self-segregation no longer made sense. The emancipated life and the Jewish tradition seemed somehow to fit very well into one another. Only some such sense of basic affinity explains, on the intellectual level, why Jews everywhere avidly took advantage of the new freedom when it was offered. Then as now there were pockets of resistance to modernity—the contemporary Hasidim being the most obvious example. In their overwhelming masses, Jews sensed that there was something sufficiently worthy about Western civilization to enable them to embrace it fully. But if the Gentile culture was so acceptable, one began to ask, why bother being Jewish? The positive pull of the Marrano role had begun.

An equally difficult challenge came from the realities involved in asserting one's Jewishness. It might be permitted, but it alienated one culturally and handicapped one personally. The Jewish religion in the early decades of the Emancipation still smelled of the ghetto. To affirm Jewishness seemed to mean committing oneself to live part of one's life in a medieval mode. Christianity, in contrast, was closely involved in the highest accomplishments of Western civilization, its art, its music, its architecture. If one wanted to belong to modern Europe one might as well have a faith that fully legitimated it. So, in the early decades of the nineteenth century there was a steady movement of Jews converting to Christianity. It was the impetus of losing men like Heinrich Heine that forced some Jews to act. They knew that Judaism did not have to mean living in the Middle Ages, that modernity did not necessarily imply Christianity. Within a generation or two they made the basic reforms in Jewish education, worship and general life style that showed how one can accommodate Jewishness to modern culture, that to be a Jew does not mean to stay in the ghetto. That act of self-transformation is mostly associated with the Reform Jews of Germany. They did indeed pioneer the new way.

However, what we have inherited is as much the work of such nineteenth-century German conservatives as Zunz and Frankel, or of such an uncompromising but modern-style Orthodoxy as that of Samson Raphael Hirsch. Jewish modernity is not the product of one movement or the creation of one charismatic leader. It is the response of an entire community to a new social situation, and as befits a people of such diversity and individuality, its adaptation to the modern world has taken many forms.

Some Jews were able to retain, unchanged, the old faith that God Himself had chosen the people of Israel to be His special treasure. Hence the attractiveness of the general culture did not affect their sense of Jewish identity. They knew why they were Jews. Most modern Jews soon lost such theological assurance. Some believed nothing, others little, and even those who admitted to some faith did so with doubts and questioning. That was as much a result of modern intellectuality as it was of coming to know the *goy* firsthand. In any case, there was little inner certainty to offset the problem of identity created from without.

The dilemma of Jewish existence was thus reinforced from

within. Without transforming Judaism to its new social context, there would have been little basis for remaining Jewish in the modern world. Yet the very act of adaptation acknowledges values in the general culture and thereby makes it difficult to have faith in the superiority, and thus the necessity, of being Jewish. Worse, to retain one's Jewishness became a special burden rather than a metaphysical privilege. The ideal of emancipation did not change certain social realities. Judaism remained a minority faith, scorned by the majority and marking as deviant all those who sought to practice it. The secular self seemed all that was needed. Thus, the old integrity of Jewish existence began to break apart. It is something of a wonder, under the circumstances, that so many Jews have insisted on remaining Jewish.

In the nearly two hundred years the emancipatory process has been under way, that interplay of pressures has been fundamental to Jewish existence. For American Jews, however, the emergence of a divided identity has been more recent. My own family history is, I think, rather typical. My grandfather, probably then in his twenties, left Sokolow, Poland (then Russia), before the turn of the century and immigrated to New York's Lower East Side. He spent the rest of his life there amidst a community of fellow immigrants. He never learned English. He didn't have to. Everyone in his environment spoke Yiddish. Though he was an American citizen and lived the greater part of his life in this country, he remained essentially a man of the *shtetl*. And he never had a problem of Jewish identity.

My grandfather finally managed to bring my father and my grandmother to this country about 1910. My father had just been *bar mitzvah*. Since my grandfather was working—$2.50 a week for cleaning up a factory loft six days a week, twelve hours a day, with a short Friday afternoon and Shabbos off—he wanted my father to go to public school, get an education and become a doctor. My father, an activist and for some years already accustomed to looking after my grandmother, went instead and got a job. He never did get to school, though he taught himself the

arithmetic and systems analysis he came to need as he became
involved in supervising mass manufacture. Though English became his primary tongue, he never gave up his Yiddish newspaper and, on several occasions when he became quite aroused
in the hectic days of the 1940's, he insisted on the right to address the Columbus, Ohio, Jewish Community Council in Yiddish. My dad lived most of his life in the essentially non-Jewish
environment of the American Middle West. He can hardly be
called a *shtetl* figure. Yet he carried with him such rich and
living memories of his youth in his own grandfather's house that
he never had a problem of Jewish identity.

I was born in New York but grew up in Columbus, Ohio. Two
of my earliest memories are of the Heyl Avenue Elementary
School. One concerns being called to the principal's office for
starting a fight with a boy named Fred on the playground. He
had called me a "Christkiller." The other one is of my going to
the principal's office to complain that it wasn't right to ask us to
sing, as we marched into the auditorium for assembly, "Onward,
Christian Soldiers." I could match those stories with others, good
and bad, from Hebrew School and Sunday school and synagogue
—but the point should by now be clear. I grew up in a Gentile
community, essentially hospitable, occasionally hostile, but always distant from the Jewishness of my family and close community. Symptomatically, I understand Yiddish well, but never
wanted to speak it. In my family the problem of Jewish identity
begins with my generation. For many American Jews it is as recent as that.

The historical record of our community makes that easy to
understand. The overwhelming proportion of American Jews
derives from the countries of Eastern Europe that never achieved
stable democracy or otherwise permitted Jews to integrate into
their life freely. As a result, the great mass of world Jewry, 80
percent of which was in those countries as recently as 1880,
barely participated in the Emancipation. One must not under-

estimate, then, the cultural shock involved in the emigrations of our forebears from the *shtetl* to "the Golden Land." Most of our grandfathers or fathers who made that transition left an essentially segregated, almost medieval, way of life, to come to one of the most technically advanced and democratically organized countries in the world. It was an incredibly long leap ahead in time and culture, and we still show its effects in almost every phase of American Jewish life. To be sure, the more emancipated Western Jewries, largely the German, had sent tens of thousands of Jews to these shores in the period from 1840 to 1880. This established a well-acculturated community that, beginning with the 1880's, found itself inundated by Eastern European Jews who arrived at the rate of a hundred thousand and more each year (the war years excepted) until 1924. Some of these immigrants had tasted the new freedom before arriving here. A minority had been educated in *gymnasia* or at universities. Others had made their way on their own into the world of general literature or politics. Nonetheless, Tevyeh and his daughters fleeing Anatevka at the end of *Fiddler on the Roof* is, for all its sentimentality, an appropriate depiction of our plight. Our families generally did not come to America from emancipated Europe but, so to speak, fresh from the ghetto.

The immigrant generation before World War I came to the United States with such a weight of Jewish experience, with lives so bound up with Jewish values, Jewish emotional patterns and Jewish memories, that no matter how American their life style became, it was still quite patently Jewish at its roots. Today, looking back at the various forms of humanism or cosmopolitanism that some of them adopted as a substitute for the narrowness of their Jewish youth, we see them less as modern universalists than as secularized Jewish types. Thus, if they were internationalist socialists who were passionately anti-Zionist, they still were Yiddish-speaking. And if they were antireligious Zionists, their language was Hebrew. Their Jewish identity went so deep in them that even when they took a stance in radical defiance, they thought, of Jewish tradition, it showed itself to be somehow authentically Jewish.

What was true of that first generation largely did not carry over to the second. They could not transmit the genuineness of their accommodation to America to their children. They, the infant immigrants or the American-born, usually did not grow up living a rich and impressive Jewish life, one whose style had been created over many generations and by now fitted in well in the social order in which it functioned. The second generation tended to regard Jewishness in America as the remnants of a European life style that was poorly adapted to the American scene. For them, to be a Jew smacked of clinging to the immigrant status they were most eager to leave behind.

The primary movement of young American Jews in the generation before World War II took the form of a cultural exodus. There was continuing flight from the ghetto and its mores, and a passion to be fully American. This country seemed to offer the opportunity, unique in centuries of Jewish history, of full-scale human dignity. The possibility of being a man among men and the promise of economic and social advancement to those who would earn it made Jews love this country dearly. Even its negative features made them eager to blend into the majority. They saw the anti-Semitism around them and even felt it function in their lives with a power that is rather different from anything the present generation of Jews knows. But they responded to it by strategies of invisibility and protective camouflage. They gladly abandoned the Judaism and Jewish style that they felt stigmatized them. Their generation had a goal: to transform themselves quickly and expertly into proper Americans. That is, to become Marranos.

To recapture their mood, to try to jump the distance to their pursuit of escape from Jewishness, it will help to note the changed significance of certain acts. If a Jew has his nose straightened today, it is a matter of cosmetics. Then it was in hope of not being identified as a Jew. If one of us Anglicizes his Slavic or Germanic name today it is almost certainly a matter of convenience. Then it was an effort to remain undetected. We greet an occasional ghetto intonation or gesture as part of your peculiar, perhaps charming way. Then it was an invitation to discrimination, or at least so one thought, and therefore one carefully trained oneself to speak without a Yiddish lilt or movement. All the old Jewish skills at survival came into play to discipline American Jews to comport themselves so that they might be indistinguishable from genuine, Protestant Americans. Once having perfected their self-denial, they were careful to avoid other Jews who, by their clumsiness with the new disguises, might implicate them in their alien ways. They destroyed what they could of their evident Jewishness, and what resisted their best efforts at retraining they repressed or denied. In their enchantment with this country they could not ask whether its good life came at too high a price or why they were expected in some measure to be untrue to their heritage.

We need to understand this style of Jewish self-denial, for it still lingers among us. We can make its changing nature clear by recalling how three famous men, each a conductor of the New York Philharmonic Symphony Orchestra, treated their Jewishness. At the turn of the century, Gustav Mahler, in order to make his way into the cultural life of Vienna, converted to Catholicism, at least nominally. A generation later his disciple Bruno Walter no longer felt it necessary to leave Judaism formally. He rather repressed it almost to the point of completely denying it. He was honest enough to say, at the beginning of his autobiography, that he was born a Jew. That was as much Jewish identity as he could admit or assume. Though a victim of Nazi persecution, Walter never participated in any Jewish activity. He hoped that if he avoided everything Jewish, people would eventually forget that he was a Jew—the sort of strategy that I sense in many people like Admiral Hyman Rickover. However, we also have Jews like Leonard Bernstein. He seeks neither to escape nor to

evade. Rather, it has seemed quite natural for him to utilize Hebrew texts and chant in his First Symphony, and though
he wrote a Mass for the dedication of the Kennedy Center
for the Performing Arts in Washington, no one accused him
of apostasy.

Bernstein's mode of accommodation is healthy. Mahler's is
clearly inauthentic. Walter's, however, is the most disturbing,
for he is a walking lie. He lived in perpetual, self-created illusion,
that he was not a Jew—when everyone knew that were he not a
Jew he would not have been in the United States. Walter, typical
of that generation, absorbed into his personality the dominant
culture's distinction between public rights for persons and its
ambivalent tolerance of Jewishness as a private though peculiar
identity. He let the society teach him that his origins defiled him,
and then he built his life on that judgment. He became a great
conductor, but he paid a high human price to become and to remain accepted.

Bruno Walter's disciplined repression of his Jewishness is a
transparent instance of a phenomenon frequently observed by
sociologists in minority groups. They call it self-hate. Because it
is generally quite unconscious, it is even more effective than conscious adaptations. Self-hate arises when the minority-group
member, who takes so many of his values from the majority
group, learns to think of himself in its terms. Because his group
is strange in their eyes, he comes to believe himself strange. Since
they look down on him, he begins to look down on himself, particularly on that which differentiates him. So, among Jews it was
truly a compliment not to "look Jewish." Similarly, in the black
community until recent years, the lighter one's skin, the higher
one's social status was likely to be. Mahler is a somewhat healthier figure than Walter, for he and his friends have no qualms
about the expediency of his conversion. But neither Walter nor
others dare mention his Jewishness.

For children of ethnic and racial minorities, self-hatred comes
as a natural part of growing up. As the child adopts the idioms,

the styles of dress and behavior, and the outlook of his society, he also internalizes its stereotypes of his people. This socialization does not suddenly stop merely because he finds himself being hurt by what he learns. He buries this negative self-image deep within him. It can come out in dramatic ways. Mahler converts, Negroes "pass." Or one can invert the devaluation of one's group by turning it against the society itself and becoming aggressively Jewish, or Indian, or Chicano. When every social or professional question is turned into an issue of minority rights, one begins to suspect that self-hate is the true motive, only now transformed into hostility against the society. More conventionally, self-hatred takes the form of dissociating oneself from one's community, often by seeking a substitute group through which one might be identified. Years back, Jews sought out Ethical Culture, Christian Science or Unitarianism as an escape from the stigma of Jewishness. Secularists preferred the alleged universalism of international socialism or the campus universality of human reason and culture. The forms varied, but the motive power was the same. The general society denigrated Jews, so they, in integrating in that society, sought to flee from their Jewishness.

There is something of the Bruno Walter syndrome in each of us. For some, even today, it is the basis of their being Jewish. Secretly they deplore the fact that they were born Jews. They resent being thought odd, even though their Jewishness is no direct handicap in their lives. Anyone who feels this way will not even be neutral toward things Jewish. His self-hatred will invest anything that differentiates Jews from the majority and especially those activities that call public attention to Jews as a separate group. It is futile to speak to him of the beauties of the Jewish tradition or of the nobility of the Jewish religion. He will not be impressed, because he cannot be. One cannot reason with him about Jewishness at all. His resistance is emotional, not logical. A man who in his depths hates himself for being Jewish needs therapeutic, not intellectual, help.

I do not think that Bruno Walter's self-denial is typical of

most American Jews in recent years. Most of us are, in this regard as in so many others rather "normal neurotics." Yet only a
few years ago there occurred one of the most dramatic instances
of Jewish inner self-conflict since the Emancipation.

Daniel Burros seemed only another peculiar youngster who
devoted time and energy to the activities of the American Nazi
Party. When he committed suicide, a study of his background revealed that he had been born and raised as a Jew. He so desperately wanted to stop being an outsider, he was so frantic to
be part of the general culture, that he overidentified with its
hatred of the Jews. He sought to obliterate his Jewish upbringing and joined wholeheartedly with those who hate Jews and
wish to see them destroyed. He was a devoted Nazi until he
found that he could not keep his origins secret. Then, more loyal
to his ideology than to his very life, he killed himself—surely the
ultimate in self-hatred. One would rather die than be Jewish.
This feeling, I take it, is the Jewish version of the psychoanalytic
death principle. If, then, there is some self-hatred in most modern Jews, we carry within us a pressure, great or small, toward
self-annihilation. Until we overcome it—and that means, first,
facing up to it—we cannot hope to live wholly and well.

I therefore have much sympathy for the concept of Black
Power. As a Jew, I know personally that one can never truly be
a person as long as he looks at himself with the eyes of those who
hate him. I do not see how Jews can dodge the fact that, religious and social traditions aside, much of the best of Western
literature from Marlowe to T. S. Eliot sees the Jew as intruder
or enemy. So, every Jew appropriating even the best of this
civilization must sooner or later come to terms with the scandal,
the disgrace of his Jewishness. And this is one reason why we
wear Marrano masks with such fixity—they enable us to escape
from our stigmatized inner selves; they proclaim us to be just
like everyone else.

If that is the primary dynamic behind our Marranohood no
amount of intellectual analysis will persuade us that we are more

Jewish within than we, on our surface, lead people to believe. If self-hatred prompts us to deny our Jewishness by identifying ourselves as purely universal men, we will not permit ourselves to see where, in fact, our values find root. This basis for being a Marrano makes analysis impossible. The need not to be Jewish will always defeat it. To those in whom self-hate is stronger than self-acceptance as a Jew, this book cannot say very much. That you are still reading probably means that you have a fairly positive attitude toward your Jewishness. But if there were no element of self-hate in you, you would probably not be attracted to a book dealing with the problem of Jewish identity. It remains one source of Jewish inner conflict for all of us, and you will have to see as we move on to other problems how much of your psyche still resists identification with things Jewish. But Bruno Walter and others—like Bernard Berenson, Walter Lippmann and Bennett Cerf—who have in public life preferred to have nothing to do with their heritage are typical not of our time but of a previous generation. We are, I think, far more Jewishly self-accepting, and that can give us the strength to look at and come to terms with what remains Jewishly negative in us. How we gained that more positive stance and what it implies for our present search demands full treatment of its own.

# CHAPTER 3

# Jewish Enough to Inquire

If most American Jews were dominated by self-hate, our venture in self-examination could not succeed. People whose personalities are shaped by the unconscious need to reject anything Jewish about themselves could hardly be expected to gain insight into what I see as even their residual Jewish commitments. Their defenses are too strong for our sort of analysis. By contrast, I find many Jews today—a minority, to be sure—taking a radically different stance toward their Jewishness. They are asking, in many different ways, "What can my Jewishness mean to me?" If we see their question only as a newly positive acceptance of group membership, we miss the quantum jump in self-understanding that it implies. Merely to like being Jewish is passive; what was previously experienced in pain has now become a source of pleasure. The new question goes far beyond that. It is not content occasionally to receive joys from Jewishness. It implies the recognition that out of one's Jewishness one might find a fundamental way of facing existence. To the people who can raise this question, Jewishness, instead of being a fate to be borne or a destiny to be endured, has become a living option.

I see two stages in the emergence of this new attitude. First, the period from 1945 to 1967, when expanded freedom made possible a joy in Jewishness that, at its heights, bordered on illusion. Second, the period from 1967 to the present, when a series of harsh realities radicalized the Jewish social situation and thus turned the question of Jewish identity from an intriguing possibility to a pressing question. While the Israeli Six-Day War is utilized here to divide the two phases, I do not believe it alone initiated a new Jewish consciousness. Its effect upon American Jews, admittedly dramatic, is best understood, in my opinion, in terms of the transition that had been under way for two decades preceding it. Moreover, its positive influence on American Jewry has been magnified many times by a series of negative experiences that have followed upon it.

The earlier, postwar era was characterized by a new sense of Jewish at-homeness in America. Anti-Semitism faded from the public scene, and as far as Jews were concerned, the democracy that World War II sought to preserve began to function properly.

The reality to which prewar Jewish self-hate attached itself was the open, widespread anti-Semitism that Jews in the United States knew in the 1930's. While Jew-baiting never achieved in America the political power it possessed in Europe, nonetheless, during the Depression years, anti-Jewish groups were openly organized and widely supported. With Father Coughlin broadcasting every Sunday over a national network and, later, with Charles Lindbergh praising Germany, the anti-Semites had prestigious leadership and little significant public opposition. No wonder American Jews trembled for their future and many devoted themselves to making their Jewishness as invisible as possible. In the postwar period there has been nothing in America to match the relative respectability of the America First Party with its barely hidden anti-Semitic appeal.

By contrast, the anti-Semites of the past two decades have appeared only on the fringes of society and have attracted few followers. The only one whose name most people can remember, George Lincoln Rockwell, of the American Nazi Party, never had more than a few dozen members in his group. The most disturbing acts Jews could complain about through the mid-sixties, were occasional outbreaks of swastika daubings, almost always the work of thoughtless teen-age adventurers. Sociologists regularly have reported that many a young American Jew has never had firsthand contact with anti-Semitism, not even by word of mouth, much less by physical act. In the 1930's, then, anti-Semitism took away in the realities of social intercourse much of the equality and dignity America had promised; it limited and compromised modern Jewish freedom. After World War II, the decline of anti-Semitism made Jewish opportunity possible, and the new openness of the American democracy made it a reality.

Educationally, economically and culturally, postwar America welcomed the participation of Jews—and a small-scale miracle took place. By the time the 1960's were well under way, the outcasts of a previous era had achieved money, status, success and power—still somewhat limited, to be sure, but breathtaking by any standard of expectation that prevailed in the Jewish community in the late 1930's. Schools that once barred Jews were happy to have them so as to have high standards of scholarship. At one point in the 1930's Princeton had two Jewish students. By the mid-1960's between 15 and 20 percent of each freshman class were Jewish, and the estimates for Yale and Harvard often ranged somewhat higher. Economically, too, the Jews benefited disproportionately from the economic boom.

In the Depression years vocational experts regularly tried to get the Jewish community to abandon its abnormal economic concentration on white-collar and professional occupations. Twenty years later, the new economy demanded the sort of educated, risk-taking, entrepreneurial style that Jewish culture and experience had created. As a result, American Jews became one of the wealthiest religio-ethnic groups in the United States—second only, probably, to the Episcopalians. With that came the emergence of Jews in every area of cultural activity. Not only were there more Jewish writers, artists and professors than ever before, but now they made no secret of their Jewishness, indeed often utilizing it in their work. I have already referred to Leonard Bernstein as a spectacular instance of this phenomenon. The pre-eminence of so many Jewish novelists—Bellow, Malamud, Roth, Mailer, Uris, Wouk and others—is an equally extraordinary development. But there is hardly a field where Jews have not made major contributions and come to positions of leadership.

The effect that this had on the inner life of the Jew, and upon his self-image in particular, is difficult to overestimate. With anti-Semitism quiescent and unparalleled freedom realistically available, the old Jewish minority consciousness no longer made sense. Jews no longer had to be Jews because the outside world needed them as pariahs, despite Sartre's famous definition of Jewishness as merely a status imposed by society. Rather, American Jewry discovered that the non-Jew would not keep Jews Jewish. The prevailing social code no longer kept reminding Jews of their inferior origins and subordinate place in things. It did not stand ready to unmask their efforts to belong and proclaim them as perpetual aliens. By and large, their Jewishness was rather taken for granted. One really had a right "even" to be a Jew.

This acceptability was, for Jews, a remarkable gain in personal freedom. It made American Jews of the 1960's the first free generation of Diaspora Jews. I do not mean to say by this that anti-Semitism is dead or that it will no longer play a role in the Jew's understanding of himself. Anti-Semitism is too much a part of Western culture for any Jew to believe that it cannot come virulently alive or that it does not need continuous Jewish communal scrutiny. As Albert Camus said in another connection, the plague germs still lurk in the most unexpected places, waiting for an opportunity to infect the unwary and begin a new epidemic.

When we discuss the second period of contemporary Jewish self-acceptance we will speak of the new "anti-Semitism" of blacks and New Leftists and anti-Zionists. But the fundamental reality of contemporary American Jewish existence and the basis of its emotional response to the recent apparent threats to its welfare is its transition from being a community subservient to a hostile environment to being one relatively free to be itself despite its minority status.

Moreover, I think the long-range prognosis for American Jews, as for other alien or oppressed groups—blacks, Indians and Chicanos, women and homosexuals—is positive. America is passing through a cultural change that emphasizes (with many hidden limits and much hypocrisy, to be sure) the individual's right to be himself. Finding one's "own thing" has become a major life goal and a justification for breaking every convention. So, in dress, in decorum, even in ethnics, many of us live in ways that our grandparents would have considered disreputable, if not sinful. When national television does not hesitate to bring into our homes numerous hippies, Yippies and far more unsavory types, one can see how acceptable the new liberty has become. If anything, this adulation of individuality is on its way to becoming the new American *Zeitgeist,* the common ideology of a culture at once empowered and oppressed by its pervasive technology.

The more the new personal freedom becomes a human reality and the less it turns out to be a fad of dress and hair style and language, the freer the American Jew will be. One would think that after centuries of ostracism and persecution, Jews would welcome this unprecedented liberty unreservedly. Not so. There seems to be a special Jewish talent for discovering threats in even the best of circumstances. As American Jews began to feel at ease, some American Jewish thinkers began to discuss a special peril to Jewish existence. Being free to affirm one's Jewishness might also mean—particularly with no significant anti-Semitism as a barrier—being free to drift away from the Jewish people. America made that particularly easy, since its pervasive secularity made it unnecessary to convert to Christianity to ground one's life in the common American way. It is not difficult to give substance to this fear. The rate of intermarriage in the community seems to be increasing with each generation and the number of young Jews who take up the burdens of Jewishness, rather than just live the good life of their peers, seems very small. The new acceptance of Jews by non-Jews may then turn out to be a mixed blessing.

Particularly since I have written so positively of the change in American Jewry's situation, I want to make my own contribution to the list of problems the new freedom brings to us. It is an intellectual version of Toffler's more culturally oriented *Future Shock*. One of the problems with openness to new ideas and life styles is that it confronts old traditions with human situations faster than it can accommodate to them. Though I think the tempo of change has increased drastically in our time, I think we can learn something of our problem from the history of Jewish efforts to come to terms with such freedom as they have been granted since the Emancipation. In the mid-nineteenth century, German Jews built their relation to the general culture along the religious lines laid down by their teachers Abraham Geiger, Zachariah Frankel and Samson Raphael Hirsch, only to have the anti-Semitism of the 1870's and beyond destroy it. So, too, in the United States the integration of Jewish tradition with the American democratic ideal worked out in the 1930's and 1940's by thinkers like Horace Kallen, Mordecai Kaplan and Milton Konvitz has seemed inadequate to the personal and religious needs of the 1960's.

At the moment it is easy to speak of Jewishness in terms of Buber's existential sense of encounter and Rosenzweig's emphasis on personal appropriation of the law. A good deal of what

I shall be saying in the later chapters of this book is my extension of their work. But I fear that by the time we work this personalist Jewishness into our community consciousness and practice, the freely moving mood of our times, made especially fickle by the need to demonstrate its freedom, will have swung to some new arc of concern. A culture emphasizing change will not hold still long enough to help us create and settle into a reasonably well-crystallized American Jewish thought style or life pattern. Instead of the formulae and blueprints of Jewish adjustments that most people want, we shall have to be satisfied with opening up the significant questions and pointing out the promising alternative answers. Then we must try them out and see what happens. We are too free for anything else. But that inability to consolidate our gains into a relatively fixed way of life is the special intellectual burden of the freedom *Zeitgeist*.

What has also been overlooked in the discussion of freedom as a threat to Jewish survival is that it makes possible a new basis of Jewish continuity. Now that Jews are, so to speak, no longer socially constrained to be Jews, they may, of course, choose to give up their Jewishness. But the same freedom makes it possible for them to choose to be Jewish in a new way—that is, to take up the fact of their birth and make it, upon consideration, the personally willed basis of their existence. Their Jewishness now becomes as much their decision as their parents' act and transforms the old familial and social inertia of Jewish survival into an existential Jewish continuity in which the self pledges its freedom to the millennial concerns of the Jewish people.

The potential virtues of such a free Jewishness may most easily be seen on the psychological level. In adolescents and young adults, coercion often evokes rebellion. Often it is not the substance of what is imposed that is resented, but the pressure. Since adulthood and maturity in our time are associated with being free to make up one's own mind, being allowed to decide against one's parents or society is a critical right. And everyone feels oppressed insofar as he is not given legitimate scope in which to exercise self-determination. A good deal of the youth rebellion is a struggle for such independence—and I think, the basis of the adult malaise centered about the question, Why am I living this way?

If being Jewish is only something forced upon one, it may have to be resisted simply as a part of trying to be one's own man. Since Jewishness carries with it special minority burdens and responsibilities, it is easy to reject Jewishness in the name of autonomy. In a society prating about freedom I do not think this is an insignificant danger. Moreover, if the emphasis on personal freedom grows in the United States, as I think it will, the importance of willing to be a Jew will increase. Obviously, not everyone in America is involved in expanding personal freedom; and in addition, traditional Judaism, like the rest of man's cultural and spiritual experience did not, until recently, have this high estimate of man's autonomy. So there will be a good part of the Jewish community that will continue to do more or less what its parents did. But, with the overwhelming majority of Jews college-trained, urban sophisticates, the impact on them of the cultural emphasis on enhancing personal liberty should be substantial. Hence the new possibility of affirming one's Jewishness as a matter of self-determination is a valuable option in the new psychosocial situation in which Jews find themselves.

More important, however, is the moral dimension of the change. Increasingly, what we mean by human dignity is the right to be self-determining insofar as that is possible. Oppression is no longer merely beatings and prison, but social forms that deny black and red and yellow men, or women of any color, the right to be themselves. Cherishing man's inner freedom, we now seek to change the forms that unreasonably inhibit it. Positively put, man at his best is man exercising his will to a useful end. To put Socrates' slogan into modern, existentialist terms, the un-self-determined life is not worth living.

By such standards a Jewishness that is only inherited is of less personal value than one that, upon reconsideration, one chooses for oneself. The two decades that followed World War II changed American-Jewish self-perception from one fundamentally characterized by self-hate to one that went beyond self-acceptance to the possibility of self-affirmation. The fruits of the new social ease were that some Jews, as early as the mid-sixties, were consciously choosing to make their Jewishness the basis of their lives. They were not many, but they were so new a phenomenon in Diaspora Jewishness and they were in such radical contrast to the dominant tone of American Jewry that they had to be taken in utter seriousness.

Since I believe it important that this change of mood be clearly understood as the background to the period of radicalization, from 1967 on, let me exemplify what took place by discussing two popular phenomena. The first is the intriguing story of the mezuzah. Most Jewish immigrants observed the custom of affixing a mezuzah to the door frame of the entry to their apartments. Aesthetically they were rather unattractive, generally little boxes stamped out of thin sheet iron or brass, but they were there. The children of these families often went on to college, where a major part of their education consisted in the debunking of their parents' beliefs, practices and values. Thus they were soon informed in their anthropology courses that mezuzahs were but another form of amulet or charm. They were a typical example of that primitive folk magic which hoped that by putting some sentences from the holy books on one's house door one could keep evil out, or, conversely, carry some divine potency with one into the threatening world by touching the mezuzah and kissing one's fingertips as one left home. The new Americans were beyond all such superstitions. So they often made the mezuzah and similar observances the butt of their attacks on the obsolescence of Judaism. Hindsight makes clear that this was also a perfect rationale for getting rid of an external sign that Jews lived in this apartment. To a generation that prized Jewish invisibility the mezuzah was a menace.

The tension between these generations then produced a fascinating accommodation. The mezuzah, once installed, tended to stay. But the arguments of the young or the pressures of living amidst a non-Jewish populace had their effect. When the painters eventually came, if they were non-Jews, they simply painted right over the mezuzah. If no one noticed or complained, succeeding painters added to the covering. There was a mezuzah—but, under the blister of paint, it was practically invisible! Minority status had exacted its toll, and the diverging generations had one less matter to quarrel over.

After World War II, however, with the massive resettlement of Jews, the phenomenon reversed itself. The new Jewish home-owners, often those very rebels of the prewar period, could regularly be observed affixing mezuzahs on their suburban homes. They now lived in mixed neighborhoods and that, of all reasons, was why they wanted their doorposts marked. It was to let their children know—I think equally to show themselves—that this was somehow a Jewish home. Suddenly it made no difference to them that all the non-Jews coming to the door—milkman, mailman, charity workers, neighbors—would see that Jews lived here. They were not concerned with invisibility but with identity. They had accepted their Jewishness in a way that was a radical shift from the prewar denials.

More, like everything else in their newly elegant lives, they wanted mezuzahs of quality, so artisans and merchants speedily responded. Today the old, stamped-out mezuzah is so rare that it is something of a collector's item for lovers of camp. Our modern mezuzahs are plastic or silver, enamel or wood, with see-through cases or an artistically distorted letter *shin* on the exterior. We do not hesitate to commission artists to make them for us, and a beautifully crafted one will be highly prized as a wedding present. No painter would dare to put a speck on one!

Yet the story has another chapter. Such self-accepting Jewish living made possible a new freedom among Diaspora Jews, for not long after suburban homes began to have mezuzahs, parents were startled when their children began asking for mezuzahs or

Jewish stars to wear around their necks. This rattled the parents considerably—a sign of the psychological distance between these generations. It was one thing to mark one's home rather privately, but quite another to proclaim oneself a Jew in one's largely non-Jewish school. The father might have worn a mezuzah during World War II as some sort of charm or identification or both, but he had long since given that up. His child's request came out of the new naturalness of his Jewishness. Other children in the community wore crosses, and so he wanted a sign of his own identity. It was as honest for him to ask for a mezuzah or a *magen david* as it was typical of his parents to be embarrassed by this assault on their barely resolved ambivalence toward their Jewishness.

My point is not that if all Jews wore mezuzahs we would have no new Marranos. Rather, I am trying to illustrate how freedom makes possible a genuine assertion of one's Jewishness or at least makes it possible to ask in a new way the question of one's relation to having been born a Jew. More specifically, once Jews freely choose to display mezuzahs, or celebrate a Seder, or visit the State of Israel, or participate in a community effort to help fellow Jews escape from tyranny, they may eventually begin to ask with growing depth, "What does being Jewish truly mean to me?" And since this question begins from action rather than speculation, since it has some existential ground, it can take on a power that changes lives from thoughtful search to commitment and deed.

This process of social acceptance and self-affirmation was so dynamic that it created a special variety of American-Jewish euphoria. Suddenly it seemed as if almost everyone worthwhile in America was Jewish, and being born into this people was a positive advantage. As one of the classic jokes of the period had it, the new language requirement for entry to Harvard was Yiddish. Popularly, the mood was symbolized by the adulation of Harry Golden. Archibald MacLeish and other non-Jewish intellectuals hailed him as a worthy successor to William Allen White.

He not only had the sagacity available only to an editor in the small towns of unspoiled America, but the morality and compassion and gusto of his ghetto upbringing. For a moment it seemed as if Harry Golden might become the new philosopher of everyman's America—being Jewish seemed that integral to life in the United States. Everywhere in the Jewish community there was a sense that we might be entering the Golden Age of American Jewry.

Then the time of radicalization began, and the Six-Day War, in both positive and negative ways, dramatically heightened what was at stake in being a Jew. In June, 1967, Jewish ethnicity surfaced in a way that no one had anticipated. That American Jews had some feeling for the State of Israel was never a question. But no one believed the emotions went so deep as to prompt significant action or that they were felt by marginal members of the community. On both accounts, the spontaneous, emotional, activist, nearly universal response of American Jews left no doubt. They still felt themselves part of the Jewish people and—at least in a moment of crisis—they were willing to make some sacrifice for their folk. Jewish morale in those days was unprecedented. Nothing in my Jewish experience, not the establishment of the State of Israel and certainly not its victory in the Sinai campaign, compared to it.

So we hoped that our awakening would mark a new stage in the history of American, indeed of world, Jewry. Then, rather quickly, things seemed to return to where they had been. By the spring of 1968, Jewish leaders were regularly complaining about the loss of spirit and the return of the old ennui. Once again the ruling law of modern Jewish existence had apparently asserted itself: emancipation leads to assimilation. Yet, as the decade ended, and surely now in the early seventies, it is clear that with the Six-Day War a decided positive shift in American Jewish self-consciousness began.

This phenomenon has usually been explained in terms of the hold of the State of Israel on world Jewry and the needs of Jews to express and assuage their hard-won consciousness of their guilt over the Holocaust. Both reasons make good sense. After nearly twenty years of existence the State of Israel had come to mean far more to most Jews than they had realized. It was so taken for granted that, like a spouse, we were no longer conscious of how much we loved and needed it. Then when the war broke out, our feelings for the State of Israel were heightened by our having realized in the preceding years how ghastly the Holocaust had been and how implicated in it our silence then had made us. Thus, the first of Elie Wiesel's influential novels, *Night,* was published only in 1960, and André Schwartzbart's *The Last of the Just* created its sensation even later. The capture and trial of Adolf Eichmann brought home how ordinary men, merely by doing what they are told and by not taking a stand against evil, do the demonic work that degrades society. Guilty at what we had not done for our European brothers in the forties, caring for the State of Israel as a precious, personal possession, we were moved by the crisis of the Six-Day War to act as Jews with a directness and commitment we had never shown before. And that, in due course, inestimably raised our consciousness of ourselves as Jews.

I want to add two other factors to that analysis. The first I have already mentioned. By 1967 the overwhelming majority of American Jews were well past the self-hatred of a previous generation and were groping toward a new Jewishness affirmed out of a new inner freedom. The Six-Day War precipitated what two decades of sociological shift had brought to readiness. It did not occur in an emotional vacuum, though only in our dramatic response to the war was it possible to see how far our community had come psychically.

Far more significant in the long run has been the new American attitude toward ethnicity. Under black leadership, various American groups have now asserted their democratic right to maintain and enhance their group identity. This is more than the repudiation of the melting-pot ideal as a maneuver by WASPs to maintain power by making themselves the image of American life, thereby relegating all other groups to an inferior status. The ethnic resurgence rather challenges the American way of emancipating its disenfranchised groups. The individual remains the legal recipient of civil rights, but his community now demands proper recognition and significant power. Moreover, it organizes itself politically to effectuate its demands. So today the Polish vote and the Italian vote are no longer a dirty reality whose existence decent Americans will deny or consider an outmoded, unhappy instrument for carrying on the democratic process. In contemporary politics, the ethnic blocs are an open, important and, in some ways, desirable feature. And, since America continues to urbanize itself, there is reason to believe that they will play an increasingly significant role in our civil affairs.

To be sure, there is nothing today remotely like a "Jewish Caucus," nor is there ever likely to be a Jewish organization that would try to guide or deliver the Jewish vote. We are too individualistic and, with all our psychic progress, too sensitive to what our neighbors think of us, to cooperate with any such effort. But in an America in which black power and Puerto Rican power and Chicano power are openly proclaimed and acted upon, it has become almost fashionable to champion publicly Jewish ethnicity. When Norman Podhoretz, editor of the American Jewish Committee's committedly unparochial magazine, *Commentary,* can join Michael Wyschogrod, one of his severest critics and a member of the editorial committee of the Orthodox rabbis' journal, *Tradition,* in making "Is It Good for the Jews?" our major political criterion, a change of mood has obviously swept across American Jewry.

To be sure, the influence of the new pluralism is probably felt among Jews more as a cultural than as a political matter. Where Swahili is being taught it is not difficult to make out a case for Hebrew, and where Hispano-American civilization is part of a relevant curriculum, Jewish studies obviously have a place. The university today shows this changing sense of cultural sophistication most clearly, but it spills over from there into our public-school system and into the arena of high culture as well.

These positive pressures to a radically heightened sense of Jewish identity—the Six-Day War; the growing inner self-acceptance; the new American pluralism—had substantial power. But I do not believe they would have been as effective as they were had not two negative forces been operating.

The first of these is the American Jew's reawakened sense of anti-Semitism. I put it that way because, for the overwhelming majority, anti-Semitism still has not become a personal experience. Yet, for most American Jews it has again become a possibility, perhaps even a threat, something that in the glow of the apparent American-Jewish cultural synthesis recently appeared unthinkable.

Again, one must turn to the Six-Day War as a revelatory moment. The critical period extended from the closing of the Straits of Tiran to the outbreak of the war. Though the United States had given assurances that it would back freedom of passage through the Straits, it took no action, gave no indication when it would do so, or what, when it was ready to act, it would then do. The other great powers, having less at stake, were even more unconcerned. The State of Israel was left to its own fate—that fact thundered in on the consciousness of American Jews. Despite all the promises and the pledges, despite the regard for and the importance of American Jews, the United States was determined to do nothing to end the threat to Israel's existence. Government spokesmen may still try to justify this inaction on the grounds that intelligence surveys indicated Israel's clear military superiority. Nonetheless, American Jews felt that they had been abandoned—by their own government.

Such aloofness is not anti-Semitism in any normal sense of the term. The move was prompted not by any hatred of Jews but by calculating American self-interest. Yet in that reckoning the needs of the Jews were not very important. If necessary, they

would—as in the days of the Holocaust—be sacrificed. For the
first time in decades American Jews sensed that they, as Jews,
were still outsiders to America. That was a shock. More, it was
a trauma, for it came hard upon a period in which American and
Jewish interests seemed closely intertwined. I am convinced that
had we not come to think of ourselves as integral to the American experience we would not have been hit quite so hard by this
desertion and by the other psychic blows that followed upon it.
Reality is often disturbing; but when it supplants illusion it cannot fail to leave us shaken.

The reaction of the official Christian bodies in the same period
was similarly disheartening. One must keep in mind that there
was no question during the war as to what most churchgoers or
their ministers thought. They sought out their Jewish neighbors
to tell them how proud they were of the Israelis. But despite the
rank-and-file support for the State of Israel, in the weeks of tension preceding the war almost no Christian organization, despite
appeals to them to take a stand, spoke out on behalf of the State
of Israel. Again, this brought the Jewish community to a fresh
sense of isolation. Again, all the hopes of brotherhood raised by
a decade or more of abrogations of the charge of deicide, of
pronouncements rejecting the linkage of Christianity and anti-
Semitism, of working together in many fields of social welfare,
particularly civil rights, seemed shattered. And here one might
suspect that there still operated some subterranean prejudice
against Jews for stubbornly remaining Jews.

Perhaps those wounds would have healed with the therapy of
time and some effort to restore mutual confidence. They could
not heal in the atmosphere of confrontation politics that now
took over. With minority groups actively seeking their rights,
particularly in the great urban areas, the Jews, most particularly
the Jewish middle class, found itself in spiritual and even physical danger. Particularly as the black community organized and
pressured to get a responsive educational program, reparatory
job opportunities and a humane standard of housing, it was often

the Jews who stood in the place they were determined to occupy. Worse, there seemed a good likelihood that the established Christian power groups would sacrifice Jewish interests as the cheapest way of keeping blacks from open insurrection.

Without some such perception on the part of many Jews, I do not see how one can understand the emotions aroused among Jews, say, by the battles of the United Federation of Teachers (a largely Jewish union) with the New York City Board of Education or more recently by the struggle over the Forest Hills scatter-site housing project. In each case it seemed as if the Jewish community had been singled out to make the sacrifice which the greater community had come to feel that it owed its long-subjugated minorities. The construction workers' unions managed to escape taking in more than a pitiful token of minority members, but the largely Jewish teachers were being asked in the name of greater democracy to forfeit their rights under a system guaranteeing employment and advancement by merit. Of the dozen scatter-site low-income-housing proposals, all those in the antiblack Italian, Polish and Irish neighborhoods were administratively disposed of, leaving three predominantly Jewish areas to bear the risks of the experiment. In both cases it seemed to the masses of Jews caught in the urban squeeze that the organizations and leadership of the Jewish community, supposedly defending their rights, had become so much a part of the urban non-Jewish establishment while currying favors from it that they could no longer stand up for Jewish rights with proper vigor.

One might suggest that these cases, taken from New York City experience, are hardly typical of American Jewry. That is true in part, for there are large numbers of Jews in small towns and some suburbs, whose lives and consciousness have been untouched by any similar experience. Nonetheless, most Jews live in the great urban complexes of America. If they are not now personally affected by the new demography and social struggle, it is only because they had the good fortune to move far enough out when, some years ago, they made their move to where they now live. Themselves emigrees, they cannot be insensitive to what they hear the Jews they left behind are going through. Thus, their consciousness too has been altered by America's social upheaval. They may be physically safe. They are not psychically as secure as they were a few short years ago.

Honesty requires the acknowledgment that there has been no public acceptance of anti-Semitism in this period reminiscent of Father Coughlin's accomplishment, much less that which European anti-Semitic political movements had a generation ago. The best one might do is point to the New Left. Before it disintegrated some time ago, its spokesmen regularly fronted for the vicious sort of anti-Israel slander that has been characteristic of Communist anti-Semitism for some years (despite its often being mouthed by people born Jewish). Today some black leaders still utilize Third World political rhetoric against Israel, either because they feel the need of a coherent ideology to structure the revolution they hope to lead or because they are financially supported by Russia or China.

Though all black leaders are under great pressure to play the militancy game and not criticize one another, it has been difficult to win much leadership support, much less any widespread mass backing, for the anti-Israel position. This is about as far as organized anti-Semitism has got. When it comes to anti-Semitism directed toward American Jews, what one can point to is the occasional viciousness of a black fanatic. That is reprehensible enough. I only wish to add that anti-Semitism directed toward American Jews is a theme rarely heard in the circles of contemporary black power though there remain places where clashing urban interests meet and anti-Semitism is a factor in the trouble. My point, however, is that since 1967 we have become increasingly aware of the possibility that anti-Semitism might yet function powerfully in American life. This perception has given our self-consciousness as Jews a jolt and charged the question of what it means to be a Jew with special tension.

To round out this picture I must sketch in here a development

to which I shall later return in some detail. I am referring to the
identity crisis that Jews and all other Americans have undergone
as part of the loss of morale that the last decade brought to this
country. The Vietnam war has largely been held to blame, but
there have been other causes as well: the dehumanizing effect of
growth and technology; the failure of character in the face of
affluence and social permissiveness; the great expectations of
American destiny and the fearful revelations of American venality and violence. In a time of extraordinary human stress there
has been no moral force in the culture strong enough to make
these difficult days a time of new insight or noble endurance,
much less of human triumph. To the contrary, it is the undeni-
able reality of a pervasive amorality in individuals and collec-
tives, economic and political alike, that has smashed an old
image of America as good and ethical, if often ineffectual. We
may have wanted our country to be less puritanical in its standards; we did not believe that it would turn out not to have very
many or very humane standards at all. The past ten years of
American history have made realists of us all. The deeper difficulty is that, with all their accomplishment, they have left much
of America cynical.

That failure of national self-confidence has had a special effect on Jews. The truth is that for most Jews the American way
has become the real faith, the effective Torah, by which they
lived. Having been outsiders to a general society so long, having
received here an unprecedented measure of opportunity and reward, they gave themselves wholeheartedly to being Americans.
I do not mean merely that they served this country on every level
of government and in every community cause, and did so in disproportionate number and with great zeal; it went far beyond
that. In that intangible realm where a culture creates a certain
style of person—"the" Briton, "the" Frenchman, "the" German
—Jews have eagerly sought to be Americans. They have done so
in the many forms that America, in its magnitude and diversity,
has engendered, and of course, with their special admixture of

Jewishness. In that amalgam, what was American predominated. Unconsciously, the average Jew tended to feel that all the good of the Jewish tradition was carried on and extended in the American ideal. So, to be a good American was, in effect, to fulfill one's Jewishness in a new and more significant fashion. This vision of tradition transformed and extended gave added power to the usual immigrant drive to settle in and feel at home.

The unspoken assumption of this displacement of devotion is that America is moral and that the American may be counted upon to be ethical. Jewish tradition may have had a far broader range of commandment, but the modern Jew was quite happy to substitute for it the presumed American commitment to moral law. The ethical American may always have been an illusion. Now it cannot even function as a public-relations image. The old dream of America's purity is gone, and we have awakened to a hangover brought on by our self-interest and self-indulgence.

As American Jewry's operative "faith" collapsed, the possibility of a return to one's Jewish roots arose. This option should not be understood as a total turn from one milieu to the other, as if somehow the change in cultural climate has started a migration back to the ghetto. What began to rise in Jewish consciousness, I believe, was the possibility of a new mix of the American and Jewish ways of life. Perhaps the subordination of one's Jewishness was wrong. Perhaps being Jewish ought to play more of a role in one's life. Perhaps—here the question touches existential ground—one ought to build one's life as an American by making one's Jewishness the foundation of one's existence. So went the new line of thought, the new sense of identity.

I recall having come across such probing in the Jewish community as early as the mid-1960's. I remember being surprised and heartened by the personal, action-oriented questions people began asking me, for it seemed to me then that the work of existentialist Jewish theology was bearing fruit faster than expected. It had taken us into the early sixties to get a respectful hearing in the Jewish community for Jewishness seen as a personal stance rather than a philosophical idea or a sociological given. And then, whether people actually understood the idea or not, there they were asking existential questions about being Jewish. My point is that the possibility of a shift in the American and Jewish aspects of one's life had become a reality to some American Jews even before the Six-Day War and the later exacerbation of urban ethnic relationships. I attribute this largely to the change in America itself that brought some Jews in a personalist time to begin thinking about what Jewish identity meant to them.

This new option in self-definition, asserting one's Jewishness, has become increasingly attractive as the American social malaise has intensified. For with every year we see with increasing clarity that the American crisis is one of values. One can choose from many alternatives the standards by which one wishes to live and yet be accepted in our society. Learned or anti-intellectual, given to force or peace-pursuing, sexually free or monogamous, altruistic or self-centered, impulse-oriented or disciplined—it seems to make no difference to America. You may be what you wish—within limits, to be sure, but limits that have been changing so as to permit ever greater diversity. Yet it does make a difference to America, as to the individual, what will be chosen, for that in turn will shape our society as it will the individual life. We cannot tell now what America is likely to become in the next decade, for in the variety of life styles available to Americans we do not see one that predominates. Worse, so many of the possibilities are built on vulgarity, infantilism and amorality that one cannot retain the old American trust that the future is bound to be better than the present.

If the old American ideal is to be revived and reinvigorated, the values that gave it power must now be supplied from another source. The culture does not somehow carry them along with it. Some independent sense of what man is and what society must become is needed if our social mood is to be transformed. The Judaeo-Christian tradition once did that for a young America, and the present crisis of values in America has therefore brought many Americans back to their Christian or Jewish roots.

For most Jews, as for most other people, I should imagine the order of the concerns is reversed. They worry more about themselves and their family than they do about society at large. The extent of our social pathology is seen precisely in that many families are worried about their chances of living what they consider decent and worthy lives in the midst of a civilization in trouble. For the Jew in this situation, his Jewishness suddenly seems quite attractive. Being Jewish, for most people, connotes a life of rich humanity and high character. The Jews may have once emphasized law, but in our more permissive time that may surely be understood as, at least, values. To be a Jew has always meant to care about how one and one's family and one's community lived. It means somehow still today books and thinking, celebrations and fidelity, industry and compassion, accomplishment and sharing, an affirmation of life and a covenant with humanity.

For an American torn by doubt and sick with uncertainty, the values of Jewish life are, comparatively, quite attractive. One's Jewishness might provide just what the environment cannot give. This insight, I am sure, is what has prompted such novelists as Saul Bellow and Bernard Malamud to give some of their most searching works a Jewish cast. They are speaking to the American situation as a whole, but the major substantive resource they can find for speaking to its condition is Jewishness. From *The Assistant* in 1957 to *Mr. Sammler's Planet* and *The Tenants* of 1971, Bellow and Malamud and other Jewish writers have worked out a possibility that the American Jewish community was slowly coming to face.

What I mean, then, by saying that the question of Jewish identity has been radicalized in recent years is that the growth from self-hate to self-acceptance in the two decades since World War II has now become a pressing matter of personal decision.

Not only are more Jews today talking about it but some small minority of Jews has gone beyond debate to action. Again this year, four to six thousand American Jews are likely to leave this country to settle in the State of Israel. In every large American city and on most great campuses, Orthodox Judaism shows signs of great vitality, not only because of its own young, but because of the numbers of people who were previously not much of anything Jewish but who, having decided to be Jewish, now wish to live it in what they consider its most authentic form. Experiments in Jewish living and action are found all over the country. In Boston Havurat Shalom, an early exemplar of this process, has survived its early success and growing pains—no mean feat—and the Washington Jews for Urban Justice have tried setting up an American *kibbutz* to meet the problems of ecology and exploitation on a Jewish basis. *A Jewish Whole Earth Catalogue* is soon to be published, so that Jews anywhere in the United States, wanting to live as Jews, will have access to the things they need or desire.

I do not know how long all this will last, and I am quite willing to admit that this turn to Jewishness may be a fad. But even a fad tells one something of one's time and its sensibility. At the moment there is an openness to being Jewish whose extent and seriousness could not have been imagined twenty-five years ago and which, even five years ago, was not anticipated. For some small group in our community, this question has been faced and answered with a commitment of self that is unparalleled in American-Jewish history. For another minority, who stand at the opposite end of the spectrum, nothing has changed in their self-understanding. They have always unconsciously hated the fact that they were born Jewish, and they propose to continue to do everything they decently can to avoid being reminded of it.

But in the middle stand the great majority of American Jews whose psychic-social situation I have tried to clarify here. In and out of the minds of many of them today flits the complex problem of their Jewish identity: How seriously should they take

being Jewish? What can it mean to them? What are they prepared to do about it? It is, of course, not one problem alone, but
a series of problems, each with its alternatives, each demanding
that we confess what it is we truly care about. But now that we
have some insight into who we American Jews are and why we
have come to raise the questions as we have, we can begin an
analysis of our Jewishness and our defenses against what I take
to be its full meaning.

CHAPTER 4

# Ethics Without Roots

The outermost layer of our Marranohood is, as befits good armor, the toughest to pierce. Many of us assert, with all the confidence that comes from echoing a widely held, largely unchallenged belief, that ethics is what really counts and that you don't need Jewish roots to be ethical. That may have been true some time ago. I do not believe it is true today—or ever was, in the way most people now mean such statements.

I know that this is a bold assertion, and I propose to spend this chapter substantiating it. It will help, I think, to see historically how the concept of a secularly based ethics gained currency among modern men and why it had a particular appeal to emancipated Jews.

Before I begin that, I think it important to clarify two matters. First, while I shall spend some time here discussing philosophy, I am more concerned with the social effect of the ideas than with the specifics of intellectual history. That leads, secondly, to the peculiarly broad construction of the word *ethics* in this discussion. While it often means the principles of right action, I must also use it to convey a whole attitude toward man, culture and the life of the spirit that was once regularly associated with it. Today we generally use *ethics* in a more technical sense, restricting it to the theory of what men ought to do. In the German milieu in which, as we shall see, the term gained its special Jewish currency, *ethics* was understood as one part, often the central part, of man's *Geist*—a term that we translate as "spirit," but which has less the overtones of "soul" than of "intellect," "being," or "human essence." In any case, for several generations now, when Jews have spoken of ethics, they have meant doing the good, but they were also using the term as a code word for a whole style of life. I shall be concentrating largely on the moral denotation of the term in this chapter, but its cultural connotations are critical to the discussion and I shall try to refer to them from time to time.

The Enlightenment that began in the seventeenth century made criticism of religion intellectually respectable and socially progressive. The rejection of the supernatural and the institutions connected with it was the corollary of the growing ability that men found they had, to explain the unknown through human reason. This was most dramatically evident in the use of mathematics to formulate laws by which the physical universe operated. In a similar way, intelligence was thought to be capable of disclosing in human affairs a universal, rational order of ethics. By contrast, revealed religion was associated with the fanatical wars then raging, with dogmatism, superstition and the Inquisition. The rational man, it appeared, could still have all the best of religion—an ordering God and an ethical imperative—without religion's many defects. He would acknowledge that the world had a Creator but would know too that men best governed their affairs through the divine light of reason rather than through the revelations and authority of the different religions.

Thus Deism came to be, and with it the charge that religion created far more harm than good, that it was a major source of divisiveness, prejudice and persecution. The wise man would be satisfied with its essence, a divinely sanctioned but rationally obtained ethics, and stand apart from its particular or institutional expression. America has a strong tradition of Deism visible among the many Founding Fathers, most notably in Thomas Jefferson. Nearly a century later, though it cannot be called Deism, the same sense of ethics as against creed finds extraordinary embodiment in Abraham Lincoln.

As the eighteenth century ended and the nineteenth began, this position was overthrown and replaced by one of radically different intellectual form, the philosophy of Immanuel Kant. This came about in response to the advent of a radical empiricism created by David Hume and others. Their thought had not only destroyed the classic rationalistic foundations of religion, but had also refuted the notion that ethics could be founded in observable, natural laws. Even worse, perhaps, they were so skeptical of the power of reason that they could even challenge the validity of the notion of natural cause and effect, thereby casting doubt on the intellectual validity of the new and growing science.

This was the challenge Kant sought to meet. He did so by identifying two separate modes of human reason, splitting science and ethics utterly apart, in a way that still troubles modern thought. To be sure, he insisted that though the two types of reasoning—the pure and the practical—were different from each other, each was as certain and as reliable as the other. Pure reason supplied the intellectual forms, like time and space, cause and effect, through which all thinking must take place. True, as Hume had said, we do not observe such forms in nature itself. But since, as Kant argued, they are the necessary forms by which reason operates, we may use them with confidence to explain nature. Thus, science is valid. The same is true of ethics, though in a separate way. Here reason is working to give laws for human conduct. Once again Kant argues that there are forms by which the mind will operate and thus, while we cannot derive ethical laws from nature, we may rely on the ethics our reason discloses as we face the situation of moral choice.

Any rational man would utilize both realms of thought, each in its distinctive way. However, man was most true to his peculiar nature when he was ethical. The other animals participate in nature, though they cannot make a science of it. To that extent, man is already different. But he is fully differentiated from them by his participation in a realm of freedom—that is, the realm of ethics. For Kant, then, not only ought scientific man to be ethical man, but he forfeited his humanity if he was not primarily ethical.

In this thinking, even God the Creator is pushed out of the picture. Where even the Deists had been able to see Him in nature, Kant said they had seen only the workings of man's mind. It is Kant's treatment of the classical proofs of the existence of God (which he showed now could prove nothing), that has made it difficult, ever since, for philosophers to utilize them. The existence of God was no longer a matter for rational demonstration. But Kant was no atheist. He moved to God by another route, that of ethics. Kant thought that, to any rational man, there could be no question of the certainty of ethics. Yet the very nature of ethics, he argued, implies certain other truths— freedom of the will, human immortality and the existence of God. These cannot be proved or rationally demonstrated. But they are reasonable postulates for any rational, hence ethical, man.

This general intellectual style, to begin with man rather than divine revelation and then move on to establish the validity of belief, was at the heart of nineteenth-century religious liberalism. In Protestantism it often took the form of Jesus as the greatest teacher of all time and the Kingdom of God as a social order to be built by loving human beings. Behind these ideas there was not only intellectual prestige but also the extraordinary scientific, economic, political and social gains of nineteenth-century progress. They seemed to give a practical demonstration of the ethical potential of human reason and helped center liberal religion on man and focus its interest on ethics. And lest this concern with ethics and reason be considered too sterile, it is important to remember that in those days the refinement of the emotions was considered an important part of developing the mind. But this aspect of man's nature could best be served by the rapidly proliferating productions of art and music, literature and theater. What intellect did not provide, culture would. The two went hand in hand, so it seemed. When one spoke of ethics, one took culture for granted, and so too the other way around.

But if ethics was the essence of being human and it was fully within the reach of ordinary reason, what need was there of church or synagogue? If ethics was rational and religion only reasonable, why dilute the primary concern of existence with a secondary, less valuable one? Thus, utilitarianism, a typical nineteenth-century school of philosophy, held that higher education, social reform and creative politics could achieve almost every significant goal of human progress. Now, it seemed clear that the Deists, by keeping a remnant of God the Creator, believed more than was necessary. One could set aside the question of creation as unprofitable and move on from there solely with ethics and culture. In some such development, there began the present reign of the secular spirit, that is, of man operating purely on the human level.

This intellectual liberalism with its democratic political overtones had a special appeal to Jews. It validated their emancipation and defined how their adaptation to the general society might best be consummated. Again, Kant's philosophic work is a useful way to approach a broad shift in the Jewish self-understanding.

Think for a moment of Kant's treatment of ethics. He had sought to lay bare the structure of reason within the ethical experience. As a result, he emphasized its orderly, universal form. A chance impulse might be ethical; but only if what one felt by

whim could be made a rule for everyone in such a situation
could one call it rational and hence hope to bring it within the
realm of ethics. To apply one's sense of duty only to some men
or to certain situations was a sure sign it was not ethical. The
indication that something is rational is precisely its being available to all minds, regardless of creed, class or race, and regardless of time, place or other circumstance. When something is
that regular, that reliable and, since it is ethical, a command, it
is best called a law. For Kant, the form which reason discloses
at the heart of ethics is the form of law. Kant is thus the intellectual godfather of all the meanings and approbation which
men have subsequently connected with the grand term *Moral
Law*.

By the middle of the nineteenth century (though Kantian
philosophy had given way to other forms of German idealism),
the ideas associated with the concept of Moral Law gave Jewish thinkers a fitting means by which to explain and defend
Judaism. Christians regularly derided Judaism as mechanistic
legalism and contrasted it with the high spirituality of Christian
love. Now Jews were able to retort: modernity meant reason, not
sentiment; and reason, in the Kantian sense, implied an ethics
whose form was law. Modern religion should be rational religion, and rational religion meant the centrality of the Moral
Law. That being understood, one could now see that Jewish law
was essentially a prephilosophic means of training the Jewish
people to the highest standards of ethics.

The nineteenth-century Jewish apologists gloried in showing
how every aspect of traditional Jewish practice had an ethical
content. Jews did not need to be Christian to be modern. If anything, they were being truer to modernity in maintaining their
Jewishness. This approach went beyond public relations and became an acceptable academic system in the work of Hermann
Cohen, who is, properly speaking, the first significant modern
Jewish philosopher. In the forty years before the First World
War, Cohen revived Kantianism as an academically respectable

philosophy and then applied it to Judaism with such brilliance that all modern Jewish thinkers, the existentialists as well as the rationalists, still work from themes he enunciated.

As a result of this general development, modern Judaism, of every sort, has a far more generalized ethical concern than did its pre-Emancipation versions, and this broad human vision has come to occupy a central place in our view of things. We often lament the failures of contemporary Jewish education, but it was exceptionally effective on this score. Almost every Jew who has left the ghetto will tell you that ethics is the essence of Judaism. In fact, it tends to become its surrogate. The regular result has been that Jews who claim little interest in Judaism are nonetheless involved in social-reform efforts in very high statistical disproportion. Secularization in our community has usually meant giving up traditional Judaism not for self-indulgence or American chauvinism but for moral activism and cultural enrichment. I suggest that this is because being a Jew has still somehow meant being commanded; only, the content has now been changed. So to speak, modernization has meant giving up Oral Law for Moral Law. But existentially, I think, the structure of Jewish existence has remained the same.

For all the value that the modern ethical outlook brought to Judaism, it also created a grave problem. We can find it epitomized in the title of Cohen's masterwork, *Religion of Reason out of the Sources of Judaism*. Note what is primary and indispensable, what secondary and circumstantial. First place is accorded to the kind of religion a modern, rational man should have. This one learns from secular philosophy. Then one looks at history and finds certain traditions leading toward this pure ideal. Cohen saw in classic Judaism an extraordinary intuition of the truths of religion of reason and an unusually effective way of making them part of people's lives.

Less loyal Jews drew some negative conclusions from Cohen's hierarchy of values. They were university men, citizens of the realm of reason. They did not need the Jewish tradition to teach them the loftiest ideals of ethics. And they knew this direct access to the truth would soon be available to most men. In a time of nearly universal higher education, we can all, so to speak, learn religion of reason as part of our general education. That makes our Jewishness, though useful, dispensable. Of course, Jewish practice would reinforce our life of ethical rationality. But if the heart of Judaism, like all religion, lies in ethical conduct, why take on the rest of the old Jewish way of life? Before philosophy had elucidated the essence of religion, that might have been necessary. Today an enlightened man hardly needs the old props.

Most modern Jews have never read Cohen, and he would be shocked at this un-Jewish interpretation of his ideas. Yet his teaching, less authentically transmitted than vulgarized into ideology, spread through the Jewish community. It was powerfully appealing. The Jews of the late nineteenth and early twentieth centuries were trying desperately to validate their place in the general society. The thesis that the central thrust of Jewishness is ethics enabled them to argue that their Jewishness mandated good citizenship. To this day, the ethical approach is the standard Jewish self-justification: Look what we have done for this city or this country!

There was also a hidden agenda in the acceptance of this theory. It let Jews be Jewish invisibly. Being ethical does not publicly identify you as a Jew. Ethical principles are, in Kant's definition, universal ones. There are no special ethical acts for special groups. Everyone ethical—Jew, Christian or unbeliever—does the same sort of thing. Now one could have what reason said was the best of Judaism, its ethics, without its disabilities, being rendered an outsider by its observance. Taken to the extreme, this view would even justify sloughing off Jewishness—that is, making a religion of ethics itself and getting rid of the nonessential and estranging Jewish forms.

Liberal Jews created the Ethical Culture movement out of this progression and long composed the greatest part of its

membership. Most Jews have not gone so far. Yet even a superficial acquaintance with most large cities (where the evidence is
easier to come by) will show that it is the Jewish liberals, generally, who are most passionate about the notion that ethics is
the only thing that counts in religion. By the same reasoning,
even those less marginally attached to the Jewish community
will say, as Marshall Sklare's Lakeville Study demonstrated, that
it is not commandments or beliefs or Israel or Hebrew that matters most in Jewishness, but doing good for mankind.

I suggest that it is the complex of notions centered about
ethics-is-really-the-heart-of-being-Jewish that has been the effective ideology of American Jewry. By that I mean that it has been
the most widespread thesis used by Jews to explain themselves
to themselves and to non-Jews. There is considerable truth in
Cohen's claim that ethics is the core of Jewish teaching; an ideology will work only if it conveys some measure of truth. Yet it
has been significant to American Jews not because of its truth
but because of its usefulness. It justified what the Jews really
wanted—membership in the society; a duty that did not segre-
gate them; and a low profile of Jewish existence. Because it
rationalized those goals, Jews of every class and every shade
of opinion have regularly explained Jewishness as essentially
ethics. Even today, though there are few exponents of Hermann
Cohen's philosophy in American Jewry, and Buberian jargon
begins to be common in the community, the ethics explanation
remains so useful that we regularly revert to it. Such is the
power of a good ideology.

Two observations are now critical to our analysis. First, this
sort of thinking inevitably tends to make the American culture
primary in our lives and our Jewishness secondary, if that significant. Since the ethics refers to all men, we can learn it better
in the American educational system and society than we can in
the necessarily limited, perhaps even clannish, Jewish school and
community. Thus we come to project a self-image of an American of broad, humanitarian interests, denying at the same time

that our Jewishness goes very deep. In other words the ethics ideology is basic to American Jewry's Marrano style.

Second, for all this ideology's high usefulness, the troubles of the American society in the past few years have been so great that it has been called into question—and with it our sense of self. I referred to this briefly in the last chapter as I tried quickly to sketch in the historical background of our discussion. I think that before 1967 some Jews had, for internal Jewish reasons, begun to seek a more authentic way of understanding their Jewishness. But positive factors rarely affect many people deeply enough to make them question the basis of their lives. I think the negative developments of the late 1960's and beyond did that, not so much the realities and fear of anti-Semitism, but the collapse of the simple ideological confidence that becoming a good American meant being a good person. That equation no longer can be taken for granted. In a society in which *Bonnie and Clyde* can substitute for Robin Hood and where *Clockwork Orange* gives us the alternatives of lobotomized serenity or violent autonomy, something is radically wrong with human values. License is no longer a reward limited to movie stars, and immorality comes in so many forms that it is difficult to think it exceptional. Americans no longer use the *McGuffey Readers* because, in fact, they know they will not live the old, alleged American creed.

But if ethics were the medium by which Jews made themselves at home in American society, an amoral American culture would make Jews feel alien. This, I contend, is what has happened. The insensitive ignore the problem and deny that anything has really changed in America. Our rightists try to restore the old American values and our leftists seek radical political changes to make ethics a living reality. They are all gambits within the old ideology. Yet, despite its tenacity, the shock of recent years has been great enough to lead many Jews to inaugurate a conscious search for a better definition of their Jewishness. This, in my view, is the intellectual root of the current crisis over Jewish identity.

To affirm America uncritically may mean giving up our values. We will not do that. We are, we now discover, too Jewish for that. Rather we raise the unexpected possibility that a return to our Jewish roots might ground the quality of life that we desire. I think many Jews find themselves in this situation, and I want to explore it with you. But we can hope for some success in that effort only if we can admit to ourselves that the old American-Jewish ethics ideology will no longer work. Only as we exorcise the old explanation we gave to our lives will we be able to move on to a fuller self-understanding. So I propose first to explore the old hope with as much realism as possible. Can we, keeping our Jewishness peripheral to our lives, still count on the American society to give us and our children the ethical values we prize?

The issue of this discussion is not whether you or other individuals will be able to lead a truly human life in our civilization. Some men will, of course, be able to do so for quite a while in our secular, technocratic world, but that does not resolve our issue. They are quite likely to be the accidental products of a materialistic and dehumanized mass culture whose norms were once permeated by Judaeo-Christian values and which still maintains a dwindling residue of them. The real issue is not individuals but our civilization itself, not whether a few souls can manage to escape the effects of our social order, but how people in general can be expected to be decent. Can we really still hope that our society will produce the character we care about?

Let us look at the primary structures shaping our society, beginning with politics. Can we expect the democratic process by itself to produce men of conscience? Hardly. The great lesson of the 1960's was that even idealists must think in terms of power. The Eugene McCarthy and George McGovern campaigns—and, in another way, those of George Wallace—were tributes to the truth that power is what counts. In politics we have learned that ethics is at best a secondary consideration. We are always suspicious when a politician promotes his cause in terms of moral values. We know that he is most likely using high phrases to cloak some naked power interest. The revelations concerning our leaders' reactions in the Cuban missile crisis, in the making of Vietnam policy, in responding to the India-Pakistan war over Bangladesh, have drilled into us the lesson that a political leader will regularly bend his conscience to conform to the needs of his office or, worse, violate his conscience to justify its policies.

When Hubert Humphrey and Chicago's Mayor Daley disgraced themselves at the 1968 Democratic Convention, we could perhaps explain their conduct by saying that the temptation of achieving great power was too much for them. But what shall we say after Watergate? Haldeman and Ehrlichman and Mitchell and the rest were in power and had little chance of losing it. Yet they abused their trust, demeaned the Presidency, and made American politics seem more degraded than anything our realism had prepared us for. Democracy is an extraordinary human achievement, but it is organized to check power, not transform it. By itself it cannot be counted upon as a major means of making men moral.

Our economic system is most easily typified by the modern corporation, that marvel of organized effort. It gets people of diverse temperaments and the most varied skills to work together smoothly. Yet the corporation is organized to produce profit, not ethics. Most executives may be relied on to avoid the sort of criminal collusion which recently led to the imprisonment of vice-presidents of General Electric, Westinghouse and several other manufacturers of electrical equipment. But General Motors was willing to pay proper attention to safety standards only after a fanatic named Ralph Nader had aroused the public and after its plan to have private detectives "get something on him" was exposed. Then, some time later, investigation showed new car bumpers designed to withstand impacts of less than 4 miles per hour!

Corporate advancement comes not from moral concern but

from fiscal creativity. The effective merchandiser will create a need no one truly cared about before, fill it with goods that soon need replacement and convince us that we must measure the quality of our existence by what we spend on his product. Certainly corporations are more concerned with social welfare today, sponsoring jazz concerts, underwriting training programs for the hard-core unemployed, endowing professorships, and such. Yet that is secondary to showing a good year-end balance. Our economic system, built on competition, devoted to profit, is in its very form designed to depreciate the ethical.

Nor, for all our vaunted American openness, is our caste system more humane. At the summit of our social life sits the club, still the symbol of having "made it," of being one of the right people. Its Admission Committee maintains proper standards. Should they be liberal enough to admit Jews, they likely have a quota; but Orientals, Mexicans, Puerto Ricans and Negroes are still largely the concern of the radically chic. Even a white Protestant who is morally aroused will have little chance of being accepted. Imagine a crusader in a club!

Admission to peerdom comes with social reliability. Even in America, conformity is a prerequisite of acceptability and conscience a stigma. If we cherish our upward mobility we had better inhibit our ethical impulses. And being poor or choosing poverty will not keep us pure. The fight to survive is so desperate, ethics becomes a luxury for the well-to-do, a set of standards imposed by those above to keep those below from getting out of hand. America is an impressively open society, but its hierarchical structure prevents it from creating high moral concern.

I think most of us know that our contemporary political, economic and social structures dispose us, at best, to live amorally most of the time. So we have trusted in education or culture to provide an antidote. The name "Harvard" conjures up a vision of the morality of learning—the devotion to the good and the true. Similarly the attraction of the Great Books discussion programs lies in our hope that if we know the best writers we will live good lives. Knowledge still implies virtue. Thus, the university, our model intellectual institution, is relied upon as the seed-bed of our humanity. The trouble is that contemporary learning is essentially instrumental so the university, instead of disseminating the humanities, turns out technicians.

No one who has been on campus for more than a few weeks can believe that he will be taught wisdom there. Students work for credits, deferments, recommendations, jobs or a good marriage, while their professors concentrate on grants, appointments, promotions, professional status, and moonlighting. No one grades students for improvement of character. Professors are not advanced for setting a moral example or giving ethical guidance. And our lower schools are typically less capable of molding personality. Instead, many of our schools serve as the staging areas for the turmoil in our society.

In another day we might have put our trust in science and relied on research and investigation to produce the humanity we long for. There is, obviously, much for us to learn from science. The chemistry of genetics and of personality disorders, the dynamics of learning and of motivation, the interrelations of groups in society, are increasingly significant to anyone who cares about mankind, for they teach us how we are shaped and conditioned as persons. They will not, however helpful they are in teaching us about the mechanisms of existence, give us guidance about its proper ends. As long as behavioral science remains strictly empirical and demands value-free investigation, how can it discover what we ought to do rather than what we are? How can it validate ethics when it insists that judgments about right and wrong are outside of its domain? Surely a major factor in the loss of American self-confidence was the collapse of our secular trust that science would solve all our problems. Yet research keeps giving man power, thus making the unanswered question of moral values all the more imperative.

Philosophy gives little more help. Kant took it for granted that man's sense of what he ought to do was unquestionably reliable and that it necessarily had a rational structure. Today both premises seem naïve and dubious. We are children of Darwin and Freud, students of anthropology and history. The commands of conscience seem to us less likely to come from a transcendent, rational realm than from the promptings of biology, class, training, culture or time. Moreover our experience of moral prompting hardly takes the form of a clear, unconditional law. Rather, wherever we turn we face relativities and ambiguity. We cannot trust the universe to be rational; hence we will not assume, as Kant did, that ethics must necessarily have a rational structure or that any rational man will make ethics primary to his existence. If anything, the radical skepticism of modern philosophy has challenged the idea that the impulse to do the good is, technically speaking, a rational one.

The situation of modern philosophy may be seen most poignantly in the life and thought of Bertrand Russell. As a man Russell was deeply concerned and personally active in efforts to make life more richly human. He was an early opponent of our hypocrisy in sexual matters and a protagonist of efforts to outlaw nuclear war. He led international efforts condemning the Soviet Union for its invasion of Czechoslovakia, and the United States for the Vietnam war. One may quarrel with one or another of his social or political judgments, but there can be little doubt that he was a deeply ethical human being. Yet, as a philosopher, he did not believe that ethics had its ground in the operations of human reason. Where Kant saw two realms of cognition, the pure, which made science possible, and the practical, which produced ethics, Russell restricted knowledge proper to that which science gains or mathematics deduces. Conscience has no standing in either, hence it has no validity in Russell's philosophy.

Russell's case is atypical of modern philosophy only in that he was so creative a thinker and so ethical a man. To read the writings of modern philosophers about ethics is a disconcerting experience. Mostly they are analyses of words used in ethical discourse, like *right, duty* and *responsible.* Or there are examinations of the logic of ethical reasoning as in sentences like "if this is true . . . then one should do that." One gets the sense of an extraordinary investment of energy and intellect, which contrasts oddly with the central fact that they never tell us why we ought to be ethical. Kant said that reason demanded it, and that unless we obeyed the moral law we were not human. Modern philosophers have no such doctrine of man or of reason. They can help us with our ethical thinking once we decide we care about something. They do not empower us through reason with a sense of, or form for, sanctions, individual or social; but, in a permissive time, that is just our problem.

Then, perhaps the arts can be counted on to provide a basis for the ethical life. In other ages the artists, particularly the writers, such as Dickens, Tolstoy, Ibsen and Hawthorne, were expected to be the conscience of their society. The only thing certain in our cultural world is that the arts have become another industry and that money comes with distribution. The result is that we are deluged with prints, paintings, records, magazines, books, movies. We consume culture; we are hardly enlightened by it. And this too has degraded most of our artists. The ones who remain honest are no longer certain what aesthetic forms are still valid, much less what ethical ideals are true. Most of them feel themselves to be most honest when they are most critical, so tearing the façade from every pretense becomes their one act of righteousness. Though this naysaying may seem to leave the creative mind free and unfettered, its reductiveness breeds a malaise all its own—moral cynicism, assuaged through aesthetic experimentation.

Thus, our writers have been unable to supply us with a new and realistic basis for human aspiration other than teaching us how to laugh darkly on the way to our apocalypse. And should there be a change, can we still believe, remembering the Nazi death-camp officials who read Goethe and listened to Mozart after duty, that even exalted cultural experiences can be relied on to induce ethical conduct?

Perhaps, then, instead of dealing with the factors which affect men en masse, we should look to the life of the individual for hope. Psychiatry has for some decades now been a major tool for freeing men from the crippling fantasies of their infancy or rebuilding lives shattered by later trauma. Today, with the old Freudian approaches expanded to include speedier and less impersonal forms of treatment, psychiatry may be even more effectively able to help the individual to cope with the trials of contemporary existence. Yet, even if it could do that with reasonable consistency—although, alas, it apparently cannot—that is a far cry from providing men with the ethical values that our society throws into question.

The older psychiatry sought to adjust man to reality, generally the reality of his culture transformed by the psychiatrist's vision of what human nature was. But reality is just what is not clear to us. It is precisely the society and its values that need transforming. And it is certainly not clear that expertise in the dynamics of inner bondage equips one to detect moral goals. Rather, many classic Freudians insisted that their work and theory were, as regards ethics, value-free. For them guilt existed only as a neurotic symptom. They did not believe there was such a phenomenon as responsible sin and hence healthy, moral guilt. Anyone who can live in our society without a substantial sense of remorse—that is, anyone who is well adjusted and reasonably happy in our world—is, by that token, ethically deprived. Psychiatry would already be doing wonders for us if it could set us free from our emotional shackles. Considering the problems it has doing that, its proper therapeutic task, we should not expect it to go on to tell us what we should do with our maturity and freedom once we achieve them.

With all this ethical impotence of our arts and sciences, there is a strong temptation to turn one's back on intellectuality and simply do what our folk songs urge, trust people and love one another. Woodstock becomes an ideal, and Esalen creates conversion experiences leading to it. Openness and sensitivity are the new way of salvation. The flower children of a few years ago and the hippies of today are only spectacular instances of a general belief that letting love come naturally could change things radically. In Eric Fromm and A. H. Maslow, the idea receives some academic credibility. The former argues that people are, in essence, good. If they could grow up healthy they would then also be decent. Not only are they maimed morally by our faulty child rearing but they are similarly injured by our competitive society. Maslow asserts that humanity has a capacity for self-transcendence and that if we study the most fulfilled people around us we too can find ways to reach their heights.

Some such sentiments motivate large numbers of our youths and appeal to adults weary of a depersonalized existence. Here the connotations of ethics broaden out into the existentialist concept "person"—and that in turn must be expanded by the new ethical adjectives "real" and "genuine." The dimensions of concern have expanded, but the thrust is, I think, quite similar. What makes these ideas appealing, strangely enough, is not the prevalence of goodness about us but the pervasiveness of evil. We are tempted to believe them whether they are or are not true. We want to believe them—better illusion than despair, so goes the message of the popular *Man of La Mancha*.

I find it ironic that secularists, who regularly used to accuse religion of fostering illusion rather than confronting brute reality responsibly, should now so often take refuge in the sentimentality of love or the goodness of human nature. Love does create a sense of value, but it also creates some of the most serious human problems. Those we love the most can wound us the deepest. Love does change us, but it does not transform most of us. We have come to expect too much of love today, which is why we are so often disappointed in it. If we did not insist that it do all things, it would have a better chance of performing its small miracles.

The problem of love is, quite exactly, human nature. If men were fundamentally good, they would not be so expert at turning something as benevolent as love into a scarifying experience.

Despite our best efforts, the one universal human trait we have not been able to hide from is the will to do evil. I am not saying that men are fundamentally bad. I am only arguing, quite in the spirit of Genesis and the rabbis of the Talmud, that man regularly chooses to do the bad, that there is something quite basic about the way he will use his freedom to sinful ends.

What Hannah Arendt saw in Eichmann, the banality of doing evil, said something about all of us. It did not take any superhuman effort on Eichmann's part to cooperate, quite consciously, in the destruction of European Jewry. He did not need to be beguiled by a demon whose promises and wiles quite made one forget his sulphurous smell. No, ordinary men find it quite an ordinary thing to do extraordinary evil. I see that truth confirmed about me day by day in individual lives as well as in social intercourse. An overwhelming burden of proof rests upon anyone who would claim that men are essentially good. No wonder A. H. Maslow made his assertions about man basing his study on a small, carefully selected sample of people who had achieved goals that he admired. Even in their case it was not something intrinsic to their nature that powered them, but insights beyond the empirical realm to which he gave the name "peak experiences." I have no quarrel with Maslow's terminology and certainly not with his sense that in dealing with such experiences we have gone beyond the realm of science. I am concerned to argue here that not only may we not look to our society to create the kind of person we care about, but so too we may not expect humaneness to arise simply from human nature itself.

One of the things that commend our young ethical activists today is that, refusing to be naïve about man, they have not let realism about how bad most of us are keep them from trying to change things. The hard-core Marxists aside, the great majority are quite nonideological. They mistrust theory because it prevents people from being persons, and that is what they care about. They even try to accomplish their ethical reforms by the most personal of means. They go and sit, or talk, or sing, or pray

—always the preferred act is one done in person and designed to stimulate other persons to something. How rare it is to see means so in keeping with an end! I share the instantaneous distaste the comfortably middle-aged feel for some of their antics. But when I reflect on the problems of moving my paunch—unless you count a donation ethical heroism and a liberal vote prophetic ardor—I must admit it is better to take the risk of occasional foolishness than to continue our collusion with evil.

But my hard-won sense of reality will not let me stop there. Can that one spark of secular morality last for any length of time when it has no deep roots? If our concern is not a family here or a commune there, but our whole society, then the personalist ethic, for all its good, is not adequate. Our civilization—let us face it—is so organized that it is not merely indifferent to morality but antagonistic. In a technological age, mass production and organization release power far greater than anything emperors could have imagined possible. The bulk of men in our society benefit from the power that technology has released and still promises. From self-interest and for our common welfare, we are determined that our technological resources shall grow and expand.

But the power of technology arises from its fundamental method of dealing with things: in the abstract, with repetition, in the mass. It knows which children are likely to succeed in college, but does not know what to do with my child's special problem; it can provide books cheaply for hundreds of thousands of readers, but has no place for works that seek a scholarly or artistic audience of one thousand. It is fascinated by means, not ends, except, of course, efficiency or better technology. It is obsessed with mechanics and tends to be oblivious to man. It is inherently impersonal and antihuman. The central social issue of our time then becomes whether our technology will be used to serve persons or whether, as we see on every hand, persons are required to subordinate themselves and their individuality to the power-producing technological apparatus.

Ethics today, then, must mean the call to defy the overwhelming impersonal pressures of our society; to shift its inhuman direction; to rechannel its enormous potential. Take any major issue of our time—ecology; population growth; the gap between developed and underdeveloped nations; the quality of modern life—to hope in any realistic way to redirect our present energies, it will not be enough to have a conscience of convenience. We cannot settle for a few general forms that most intellectuals can be counted on to follow. Nor can we await an occasional spasm of the will that says, "You really ought to get involved in something."

Meeting such issues is not a one-decade project, and reordering our civilization as a whole will require more than a feel for morality. It demands moral stamina; moral fiber; moral endurance. To mean anything today, conscience must be tough enough to stand up against the incredible energies that society regularly brings to bear against its demands. It must be committed enough to work for long-range goals that demand great effort and even greater patience. It must be determined enough to bear suffering and setback and yet refuse the ultimate victory to a world of hardheaded realism. That is the only sort of ethics worthy of the name in our day, and secular civilization shows no promise of producing it, not even among our youthful idealists.

Before the Cambodian incursion and the Kent State killings the number of socially concerned students, including those who at one time or another may have signed a petition or tutored a disadvantaged child, was about 20 percent of the campus population. That means that during the years of greatest student involvement 80 percent of our students did nothing. Now that the 1970's are upon us, campuses are relatively calm and complacent. The passion for man, apparently, recedes that fast.

What our society is producing en masse is not ethical men but the new realists, men whose approach to life is, in the last analysis, cynical. They know that society cannot be bested. To join the system means to be ready to pay its price. So, they will perpetuate their adolescent freedom as long as they can, until the time comes when they sell out; "doesn't everybody?" The responsibilities will crowd in fast enough. Meanwhile, gather such pleasure as you can. "Maximize the kicks. Stay away from causes"—maybe even love. Keep uninvolved as long as you can. "Sit loose, ride easy, play it cool."

That is the attraction of marijuana. It provides instant satisfaction and doesn't bother anyone else; escape and fulfillment, all at the same time. The drugs appeal because what most personalism comes down to is our pleasure. Being alive becomes having feelings; the more sensation the more life. And if illicit chemotherapy is too radical, there is always the dream of unending play, say twelve months of surfing, dependent on nothing but a good wave.

Our civilization is creating a new paganism. Outwardly we are elegant and assured, as befits our growing wealth and increased experience. Inwardly we are becoming as empty as the ancient Greeks and Romans came to be. With nothing finally to trust in, with no sense that there is a right by which to live, how can we, day by day, find some lasting worth and dignity? How shall we keep from despairing about the value of existence? As long as our standards are limited to the scrimmage of our appetites or the promptings of the media, we shall have no ethical drive and hence no security of self. For the essence of ethics is not compliance with the promptings of biology or the urgings of society, but their transformation in terms of what we know ought to be. Moral concern arises from a transcending ideal and its concomitant command. Without that vision of what must be, we are condemned to what is and its variations. Without the sense that by our being human we are called to overcome what we have been and done, we are lost in the practical and the realistic.

If we are to hope to change our world, or simply rescue it, we cannot settle for utilitarian arrangements. It is just what constitutes utility that we are fighting about. Nor can we rely on the fact that most intellectuals still have some sense of conscience.

Our situation demands more than moral inclinations. It needs ethical devotion, stubbornness, persistence. Were it not a contradiction in terms, I would say we need ethical fanatics. Yet, without the blindness, it is just such a sense of ultimate concern that we require. Anything less central to our existence is not worth calling ethics.

Today, we cannot expect to motivate that sort of ethical sense simply by being part of contemporary society. Halford Luccock once called such an attitude the cut-flower theory of ethics. We love the blooms, but we don't see the need for roots or foliage, or the virtue of tending a plant until it comes into bloom, or the importance of its producing seed. But we will not long have flowers without all the rest that goes into gardening.

If we are to have an ethics that can challenge and judge, contain and redirect the amoral and immoral powers in us and in our social system, it must come from a source beyond our society and ourselves. Since we are the problem, we cannot be the solution. Only when our ethics arises from some transcendent moral ground can it hope to mandate our unceasing, unrelenting, unending concern to make everything human come under its sway.

And that, it seems to me, brings us to the first crux in our analysis. The values we hoped to realize more fully by sloughing off our Jewishness and embracing general culture we will no longer find waiting there. We must bring them to the culture if we would have them. And we must be committed to them with some strength if we would maintain them in an amoral, often immoral, world. If then we still care deeply about that sense of life which was symbolized in the word *ethics,* we must give up our old ideology and its concomitant self-image. If we are to have ethics we will need rootage somewhere; and for most Jews, I contend, those roots are their Jewishness. Hence the old picture of "very much an American, very little a Jew" is wrong. It was a Marrano portrait, showing only our obvious adaptation, concealing tightly the old self within. But, having clarified what we are not, it is time to begin to see what, in fact, we are.

# CHAPTER 5

# Finding a Worthy Minority

The next Marrano strategy we must examine is closely allied to the previous one, for it says: Granted that I ought to search for roots to my ethics. But isn't that a private matter? Why should that involve people and groups? And, of all groups, why the Jews? Surely you don't have to be Jewish to be ethical!

This last assertion is surely correct, logically speaking. Ethics being universal, any human being can be ethical. But one does not need to be a student of Kant to know that. The Bible knows of righteous Gentiles—Noah, Jethro and Balaam, to mention a few—and the Talmud contains the sweeping dictum that the pious among the nations of the world have a share in the life of the world to come. The question is not one of theory, whether one could find one's ethical roots elsewhere than in the Jewish people and its tradition. Rather, when the one who asks is a Jew, it would seem to be one of fact, whether the inquirer has not already derived many of his values from this community. Thus, in

his quest for rootage to his ethics, should he not first see how
deep his stand within his community's values goes? Let us, however, in proper analytic style, begin first with the general problem of group association, and then we can return to the special
case of the Jewish people.

Ethics is founded on the individual and his free decision. To
surrender one's autonomy to a system or a group is to forfeit
much of one's humanity. Fascism, Communism and the lesser
tyrannies of our time have made that a matter of public observation. Even groups whose ideology does not demand surrender of
the individual conscience eventually pervert it. Political reform-
ers end up serving the party's or power's ends rather than the
people's—so Hubert Humphrey—and labor leaders who decried
the heartless, entrenched power of the industrialists wind up defending their own establishment—so George Meany.

Who has not had the experience of joining other idealists to
improve education, open a clinic, or save a neighborhood, only
to see the early joys of shared purpose degenerate into politics
and bureaucracy? There is something about bringing people together that in itself works to subvert our ethical impulse. So,
desirous of staying pure, we adopt a tactic of withdrawal, spiritual *à la* Zen Buddhism or Hindu meditation, or practical *à la* the
good life in metropolis or the natural life of man in the wilderness.

Solitude can renew our humanity, yet its worth is limited by
the interdependence of human beings. I mean that not only in a
practical and economic sense, but in a psychic one as well. Some
rare specimens of our species become more fully human by being hermits. For the rest of us, Genesis' reason for the creation
of woman remains true—"It is not good for man to be alone." I
believe it is the ultimate aridity of solitude that makes us so
desperate as, in our unsatisfying time, we search for fulfillment
in love and family. And rejecting the notion of man for himself,
many people will then limit their moral concern to those they

love—including perhaps a few neighbors and friends. They are enough of a burden for most of us. If you include many other people, the problems become too great, and ethical failure becomes too certain.

Ethical devotion to one's family and one's neighborhood is surely a sign of true humanity. But it is not all a man ought to care about. Here I think we may take our cue from perhaps the greatest teacher of interpersonal relations in our time, Martin Buber. His little book *I and Thou,* now fifty years old, has become a classic for illuminating the way in which one becomes a person by entering into relation with another person. Without such "I-thou" encounters, people remain part of the world of things and objects; with them, we discover who we truly are and what we ought then to do. Because of Buber's great emphasis on what can happen when two people are open to each other, many an enthusiastic convert to his views has argued that one other person is all man needs for fulfillment. This notion is a distortion of Buber's teaching. His understanding of man is based on the "I-thou" relationship, but that in turn culminates in his view of community.

Buber stresses man's social nature. On the simplest level, man cannot achieve humanity without relating to an other. But he is part of mankind as a whole, with a responsibility that reaches out to all of them, even as he shares with all of them the unique potential of being a subject in an encounter. What two can share, so may larger numbers when they reach out to one another. Such encounters have occurred among small and large groups in history, and making communal encounter the reality of man's existence is humanity's messianic task. Hence, Buber taught the necessity of reaching beyond one's love and one's friends to one's people and one's nation and ultimately all mankind. Any lesser sense of duty and goal rendered the authenticity of our openness to others suspect. He worked out these ideas in many books after *I and Thou* unfortunately not often read by "I-thou" enthusiasts.

Moreover, this did not remain mere theory with Buber. He worked politically for its accomplishment through his lifelong devotion to the causes of religious socialism and Zionism.

I find Buber's teaching and example fully persuasive. It explains in a modern way the ethical synopsis that Hillel uttered two thousand years ago: "If I am not for myself, who will be? But when I am only for myself, what am I?"

When our ethical horizons extend progressively from family and community to include finally all mankind, it follows reasonably that we cannot hope to meet our ethical obligations alone. The greater the task the more we need to associate ourselves with others to accomplish it. No man, no matter how great, by himself ever changed a society. The great statesmen had many followers, the great religious leaders disciples and then masses.

I think it highly instructive that the previous decade, which produced unprecedented interest in individualism, should also have produced a new concern for community. To take a homey example, the fashion explosion, which multiplied the possibilities of acceptable clothes styles from "mini" to bizarre, made one an individual against conventional forms of dress only to create a new group of conventions. Mustaches, beards, sideburns and long hair are less a sign of who you are personally than of with whom you wish to be identified. The hippies were individualists, but they preferred congenial neighborhoods to being hermits. Today, quite significantly, they have started a movement toward communal living.

The longing for individuality, about which we hear so much, is at the same time a longing for a different society, one of openness and love. Existentialist self-concern is not the whole story; and this feel for community is a good part of the reason, I am sure, for J. D. Salinger's losing his appeal. Out of our new individualism has come, strangely enough, the new politics of participation. We have come to recognize that for us truly to be persons we must join with others to create a society congenial to all persons. We become more our true selves, and not less, when we participate in large groups and mass movements whose goals, whether the assuring of civil rights or the reducing of air pollution, have been conceived as contributions to the enhancement of life for everyone.

The point, then, is that ethical concern implies group association. The question next becomes, Which groups?

Whatever they are, they will be minority groups, for that is the ethical reality of man. The mass of men do not care about the right for very long, and a substantial number are willing to do a good deal of evil much of the time. The overwhelming majority of people always prefer to leave things just as they are. So, moral improvement is always a function of minority groups.

Since I propose, in due course, to apply this general line of reasoning to the Jews, permit me a few more words on the importance of minority existence. I am not trying to argue the theory of cultural pluralism, that we owe it to America to enrich her civilization by keeping alive our ethnic groups and their customs. To an immigrant generation, that was a valuable idea, for it validated their obvious difference from the established culture. Even now it has some appeal as encouraging resistance to a culture of WASP conformity, once politely called the melting-pot theory.

If cultural pluralism means that ethnic groups should maintain their identity for the sake of the society, which might otherwise be deprived of a St. Patrick's Day Parade or the Syrian bakeries which still make flat bread, then I do not find it morally compelling. The extent of variety in our society can only be a secondary consideration when I determine how I should live my life. And if maintaining my ethnic community would mean preserving the burdens and disabilities it confers, then the modest social gain would be more than offset by the personal problems it engenders.

However, I hope that today cultural pluralism means that our society recognizes the virtue of ethnic groups' prizing their own ethnicity. If blacks wish to live out the beauty of their blackness or Puerto Ricans find their Caribbean heritage of continuing worth despite residence on the American mainland, our culture welcomes their participation and their difference. This is a simple recognition of the right of ethnic self-respect. It is, as a result, a highly ethical attitude.

I want to carry the argument for group difference one step further. I am urging it not only for what they may want to preserve in that group, but as a way of dissociating oneself from the dominant culture. Minority existence is a positive way of dealing with one's alienation from what the mass of our society is content with or willing to accept. Whatever your standards—cultural, intellectual, ethical, human—American practice will drive you into some sort of minority group in the hope of preserving them. Otherwise our civilization compels us to expertise in mediocrity. It operates by sheerly quantitative standards and its great rule is: the more the better. It spurns the higher range of interests and tastes and appeals relentlessly to the so-called mass audience, the consumer public. Television is the showcase of our taste. Though most television shows are aimed at dull and childish minds, most Americans appear to be happy with most television shows. What alert and sensitive man will wish to identify himself with such a majority?

To shift from the realm of consciousness to action is also to focus on relatively few people indeed, for only a "saving remnant" works to change things. Americans may be quick to complain, but they are, despite our penchant for volunteer organizations, slow to change the way things are. Try getting people to visit shut-ins or to beautify the community, and you are likely to end up, if you are lucky, with the same handful who cooperate in other activities. If, then, ethics implies action, every ethical person will choose to be part of some significant minority and willingly take on its duties. Such membership will be important for him just because it separates him from the mass, and he will be faithful to it, for only in that way can he be true to himself as an ethical being.

I assume that every caring person will be a member of many minority groups and active in some of them—working to clean up our rivers, promoting inflatable sculpture, leading an alumni association's development-fund drive. There are many worthy causes. But since we are talking about the centrality of ethics to existence it is important that we gain some sense of hierarchy in our affiliations. Some groups are more important than others and should receive more of our efforts. Some movements are more significant to us at one stage of our lives or at one point in history. But some are as lasting as the human situation.

Those activities which, throughout our lives, seek to make and keep us moral individuals and improve our society are worthy of the highest priority. And those groups which have sought to keep men faithful to ethical truth and preserve that insight through all the vicissitudes of history should be basic to all the rest of our lives and activities. I do not say that they are the only groups we should associate with or that we should give them all our time. It is pre-eminence, not exclusivity, that concerns me. Our humanity hinges on our ethics; hence we should give pre-eminent allegiance to a minority group that will sustain and enhance them all our lives long.

One step further. We must not forget the problem of ethical persistence. Considering what man and our society are, the ethical task is not short-range, but messianic, in scope. The last decade saw great ethical activism, but what will keep its positive thrust going? There is little in the motivating forces created by our society, except disgust, to awaken and empower long-lasting and broad-based movements for social improvement. The cynics see protest as merely the present generation's panty raids. The sympathetic worry that the overexposure of demonstrations and the overkill of activist rhetoric will bring on repression or that the frustration of exaggerated expectations will lead to apathy. There are also many indications that the more lasting drift of our society is to the amorality of pleasure-seeking and self-indulgence. There needs, then, to be something in our lives that persistently renews our commitment to the ethical, some group where our moral stubbornness is strengthened and at the same time given effective expression. What we cannot do alone we accomplish here together; what we do not complete in our lives, that group will carry through to completion.

There is no group whose record of continuing devotion to ethical excellence, whose moral persistence in the face of the most inhuman treatment and whose stamina in pursuit of the humane, is greater than that of the Jews. Any man whose concern for morality goes very deep ought to honor their achievement and, if he is without similar roots or an equivalent community to empower and fulfill his ethical striving, consider joining them. But if one is born a Jew, is already part of that group, has already in some way been shaped by their historic continuity, he ought to recognize that the roots of his own ethical stubbornness almost certainly stem from his Jewishness.

Over the centuries being Jewish had much to commend it ethically. But in our time Judaism has a unique emphasis to add to all its traditional virtues: responsible alienation. It teaches one withdrawal without abdication and distance with duty. This is an unparalleled approach to reforming society. It is what Western civilization in its time of moral decline most requires and what Jewish tradition and history have made central in the Jewish way of life.

Jewishness as alienating is a primary datum of Jewish experience. What is unusual and precious about the differentness it inculcates is its correlative positive concern for other men and society. The danger of most contemporary alienation is the sort of character it tends to create. The modern men of the novel or the film tend to be either detached and enervated or revolutionary and violent. The first type is so disgusted by what his distance from society has made clear to him that he refuses to get involved on any level, thus creating another social ill, the unfeeling, untouched person. The other type is similarly revolted by what he sees, only he turns his anger into an assault on the social order, caring less about what will be than about the need to be rid of what is.

Without alienation, we accept the status quo and thus co-operate in perpetuating its evils. Alienation enables the prophetic judgment to be made; but how, then, can one love what one has condemned, caring for it enough to return to transform it? From Moses to Malachi, from the Pharisees (literally "the separa-tists") who shaped rabbinic Judaism to the leaders of Diaspora communities like Samuel ibn Nagid in Spain or Josel of Rosheim in Germany, the Jews have practiced that paradoxical stance: radical social judgment combined with commitment to better-ment from within.

Let us take a look at what a Jew stands separate for. It is, quite simply, to be reminded of the values of his people, to be renewed in Judaism's high sense of what a human being ought to be. The Sabbath, even in partial observance, is a rejection of the coercive American sense of time—which is most clearly seen, I think, by observing the compulsive way most Americans use their Sundays. To celebrate Shabbos is, by that fact, a declara-tion that one refuses to be bound to the normal patterns of this culture. Its strangeness helps to liberate one from the oppression of the daily routine and turns one instead to family and books, to prayer and rest, to being one's own man. Jewish study is hardly utilitarian—our joke is that we do not want our sons, much less ourselves, to be rabbis. So to sit with the Bible or peruse Jewish literature is, by that act, to reject the usual Ameri-can emphasis, that education is for use or gain.

Such study directly encourages social transcendence; for rab-binic literature, to take an easy case, speaks of Persia and Rome and Greece and Judea, of kings and slaves, of vats of wine and jugs of olive oil. For a moment we are in another world, and then a comment about losing a child or being just to our day laborer sends us back to our own time with new and broadened perspective. Or, again, participating in decisions about the local aged, the insecure in Chile, the oppressed in Russia, the embat-

tled in the State of Israel, involves us in the real problems of ap-
plying ethical ideals to social reality. Most Americans do not do
such things. They do not have this range of moral activities thrust
into their consciousness at an early age. But for two thousand
years or more this is the sort of thing Jews have separated themselves from society for. Animating the Jewish way of life has
been the passion that every Jew should have the fullest chance
to be a decent person.

I put that in personal terms, but it should be balanced by the
insistence that each community strive to be a model of social
righteousness. There is no tradition of monasteries or nunneries
in Judaism. The closest thing Jews knew to living out a rejection
of society is the Essenes, the purported source of the Dead Sea
Scrolls (though the Essenes were pacifists and some of the
Scrolls are militaristic). They moved out of the Jewish community to the Judean wilderness, largely because they were determined to protect their spiritual purity against the corruptions of
normal society. They thought of themselves as Jews and wanted
to remain within the Jewish tradition—to save it from corruption,
of course. But their way of life was so deviant an interpretation
of Jewishness that they died out, barely leaving a trace in Jewish
literature. Were it not for Josephus' and Philo's interest in telling
the Gentiles of the first century about the curiosities of Jewish
life, we would know little about the Essenes.

No matter how negative one's judgment is of Sadducean Judaism in the same period—and our understanding of the Sad-
ducees is entirely dependent upon the documents of their oppo-
nents, the Pharisees—they did not run away from the moral
problems of a society growing more complex. Their Scriptural
orthodoxy may have been too rigid in the face of great social
changes, but they were there, in Jerusalem, worrying about Romans and taxes and laws of purity and the sanctification of everyday life. Such a refusal to turn from the realities of politics
and trade and passion and to save values for a special depart-
ment of existence has been the customary Jewish way. Even

Jewish mysticism reveals it. The authors of the mystic classics were all community figures, not hermits or recluses. And when in Hasidism mysticism began to affect large numbers of Jews, the inner experience was brought into the everyday life of business and family, not limited to spiritual exercise or theosophic speculation.

Concern for the fulfilled society is already one of the distinctive traits of the Biblical experience. The Covenant is made with the people of Israel as a whole, not with a characterless aggregate of private individuals. Its commands speak not only of good men and virtuous families, but of a folk that is to be "a kingdom of priests and a holy nation."

In the Diaspora the Jews implemented that same social-ethical vision through communities to which a considerable amount of autonomous political power was given by the general state. In Babylonia the Jews were virtually a nation within the nation. By royal decree, they independently collected taxes for the king as well as for their own community, regulated their markets, and operated the courts by which they settled all manner of litigation. Later, in their communities scattered throughout Western Europe, a similar ethical order is everywhere evident. Despised by the Gentiles, Jewish life nonetheless always meant due process before just courts, the honest mediation of disputes over rents and loans and partnerships, care for the sick, hospitality for the traveler, the use of appropriate force to contain the unruly, and the fair apportionment of the heavy levies required by rulers whose main interest in the Jews was for their money.

Why were the Jews throughout the Middle Ages successful in international trade far beyond what we find among other peoples? The answer is to be found not only in necessity and in the dispersion of family and folk, but especially in the transnational character of Jewish language and Jewish law. A Jew in Amsterdam who had a cousin in Constantinople who was married into a family that came from Venice had many advantages in doing business through such relatives. Not the least significant of these

advantages was the knowledge that if, as may happen to the closest of relatives engaged in business together, there was a lawsuit
among them, they would be under one law. Regardless of which
city's Jewish court they came before, the provisions of the law
would be relatively uniform and the standards of justice com-
parably high. Talmudic law is from the beginning international;
Babylonians living under Parthian rule created the official interpretation of a code compiled in the Land of Israel under Roman
rule. And wherever the Jews went, the Talmud went with them.
The Rothschilds were, in due course, made possible by all those
preceding generations in which no local Jewish court ever lost its
universal character.

This phenomenon is not merely of historical interest. It has
been an intrinsic part of the Jewish life style passed on from
parents to children down to the present day. Only in recent times
have Jews been free to apply their social passion to the society
at large. But that they are devoted in overwhelming numbers today to all manner of causes to improve human relations goes
back to the academies of the Pharisees, the marketplaces of
Babylonia and the community councils of German ghettos and
Polish provinces. Each modern Jew is personally heir to that
diverse tradition. Millenniums of teaching, preaching, practice
and expectation make him, so distinctively and disproportionately, a socially committed person. He is motivated, whether
consciously or not, by a mentality that has developed through an
unparalleled assortment of life styles, all of them seeking to
create moral communities founded on family loyalty and personal rectitude.

Nowhere is the shaping power of Jewish history, faith, culture,
experience, will, as these mold men and form a society, more
evident than in the State of Israel. This is not because Israeli life
has no moral flaws and no great human problems. The Israelis
are still part of history and share its pervasive sinfulness. But
what they have done with political power—the best index of a
nation's ethics, and usually the most disgusting and dismaying

one—has been, by comparative standards, extraordinarily just. Without experience at statecraft, with no oil, copper, uranium or natural resources to provide a base for economic viability, and with the need to improvise and innovate from one problem to the next, men from North Africa, from India, from Western Europe, from Russia, from South America, from the United States, Jews of every physical and cultural type, have worked together to create a democratic, cooperative society, the like of which has seldom been managed elsewhere in the world.

It was fate more than will that brought most of them from their diverse backgrounds to the Land of Israel. But none of the external forces that drove them there or that have continued to threaten them could have imposed on so diverse a group the sense of unity and moral purpose that characterizes them. Rather, it is their awareness despite their differences, at times sharp ones, that they are all Jews. They have had little success defining who is a Jew or what Jewishness consists of. Yet they know their state must reflect Jewish values.

If any group in history should have felt alienated from mankind and insisted that it was time to give up the old Jewish passion for decent men and just societies, it was this mass of tattooed, scarred, debased and bereft Jews. In the teeth of disaster their Jewish moral stubbornness reasserted itself. They would not let vicious men destroy their ethical devotion. They would not stop trying to be human in an inhuman time. Out of such magnificent, persistent, Jewish maladjustment, against the obvious lessons of the age, they have tried to build a state that is humane. The State of Israel has often fallen short of that goal. Even a superficial acquaintance with the Israeli press shows how aware the Israelis themselves are of this. But that the State of Israel has succeeded ethically as much as it has is what makes not only its citizens but its visitors and observers rejoice in this startling expression of the old Jewish spirit.

Being Jewish is, for all its historic overtones, a very present thing. When, then, I meet a Jew who tells me his ethics have nothing to do with his Jewish birth and upbringing, I cannot deny that that is possible, but I suspect that the truth is that he is a modern Marrano. I know of no way to prove that that intuition is correct. It is another of those questions that one must examine within himself. But I can point to certain social data that should be taken into account. If you ask most activists of Jewish birth whether their Jewishness has anything to do with their ethical passion, the response is generally negative and frequently scornful. Yet almost every survey of such groups has turned up an unreasonably high proportion of Jews among them. There is no logical way of moving from the statistical probability to the causes of an individual's motivation. Still the fact remains that, for many years now, in Europe as in the United States, one of the most predisposing factors of social activism is to have Jewish parents.

This reality is usually discredited merely by taking a superior intellectual stance of universal, rather than sectarian, ethical concern. One's duty is to rise above "the idols of the tribe" and concern himself with those men most in need, whoever and wherever they are. From such a perspective, to work for a Jewish cause is insufferably parochial. Even to organize a Jewish effort for a general human cause is embarrassing, if not immoral. This insistence on being humanitarian as men, not as Jews, can lead to strange lengths. I have known people who react instantly at the first news of a massacre in Burundi, Bangladesh, the Sudan or the Congo; who remain incensed about the apartheid in South Africa; who espouse the virtues of American Indian culture; who enlist to preserve the rights of Mexican-Americans—and ignore the plight of Russian Jews. They are interested in the welfare of every oppressed people but their own. By the same token, they also fail to see that a good many of their fellow-traveling humanitarians are also Jews. Such selective ethical vision is typical of the Marrano.

The academic variety of Marrano provides another paradox of group identity. Many Jews have chosen academic careers at least partly to escape the normal ethnic and class distinctions. Their hope has been to live in a select society centered about the universal concerns of intellect and culture. Yet these Jewish professors generally prefer to be at the larger universities. This turns out to be not merely a matter of prestige and facilities but of companionship and sociability. The smaller, less cosmopolitan campuses do not provide the peers and the style, the savvy, sophistication and irony that they enjoy. When they do find a circle that they are intellectually and culturally happy with, it generally turns out that most of its members were also born Jewish. They may associate with one another ostensibly in terms of their mutual universal interests. They are, in fact, a special form of Jewish community. Indeed, their pattern is so distinctive that it often wins a few non-Jewish members who enjoy sharing a derivative Jewishness, including, inevitably, a few key Yiddish expressions.

Whether activist or academic, these Jews are most easily understood as Marrano types. They use the moral claim of the human community as a rationalization for their unwillingness to associate with the Jewish community in which they were born and, likely, raised. Yet the fact of their Jewishness clings. Were they not Jews, they would not require their characteristic ethical or intellectual justification for their new style of existence, nor would they find themselves so comfortable with others similarly devoted to a messianism and intellectuality that still evidences its Jewish roots.

This form of Jewish escape also occurs, in existentialist guise, as the assertion of radical individualism. With autonomy and freedom the basis of personalist activism, the effect of social conditioning is easily underestimated or denied. This is a particularly attractive possibility for Jews with their strong antidogmatic, antihierarchical training. From our youth we are taught that Jews do not have creeds. In matters of faith we leave many options open. Our specialty is rather interpretation and argument. The master is entitled to respect; but, above all, he cherishes a good question. And traditionally, age will always give way to learning.

In such a community there is great encouragement to individuality. But the Jew who becomes doctrinaire about autonomous personhood and denies that he has any relation to the life from which he comes is likely to be fooling himself. Indeed, a whole tradition of jokes has grown up around this evasion. For example, a comedian was doing a telethon for a worthy cause and taking calls. He was stunned to hear a voice say, "Are you Jewish?" He finally managed to recover and say, "Sir, it is one of the glories of the United States of America and its democratic way of life that its citizens are judged on the basis of their personal character and performance rather than in terms of their race, creed or class." To which the retort was, "Oh, so you are Jewish."

Individualism is a major index of our humanity but social patterning is no lie. The Marrano thinks his Jewishness is hardly noticeable, if not invisible. That is true for him, but hardly for most other Jews. Despite his talk about humanity as a whole or radical individuality, his very Marranohood identifies him as a Jew. Logically, he need not have, and perhaps does not have, any significant inner ties to his Jewishness. But even the patterns and style of denying one's Jewishness testify otherwise. They say that, despite our negativity and repression, our Jewish origins still influence the shape of our lives. Though that is neither always so nor fully certain, it is generally true. Given our values, our Jewish roots seem clear.

I am not suggesting that you accept Jewish minority status because you were born into it, but rather that you consider freely choosing to affirm it as consonant with what you know to be most true about yourself. If your first impulse is to dismiss the possibility that, at your core, you retain some set of self that is distinctively Jewish, I think you ought to ask yourself whether some residual Jewish self-hate is making itself felt. Perhaps you resist the suggestion because you do not wish to be dissociated from the American majority, or you bridle at any hint of coercion, even that of birth within the Jewish people.

But if you are particularly disturbed that it is your Jewishness that is being urged as the basis for your difference from others, I think you owe it to yourself to probe your feelings about your being a Jew, especially the negative ones. For most American Jews the ethical style they affirm would seem to make the Jewish people a particularly valuable group in which to refresh and through which to effectuate their values. And that assertion leads us to continue this analysis by discussing the extraordinary social instrument by which Jewish values are transmitted and the Jewish sense of character is formed.

# CHAPTER 6

# The Power of Being an Ethnos

The next line of Marrano defense is a protest against the practicality of the notion that our Jewishness can still have forming power in our lives. After all, the argument goes, we're not very Jewish. We don't go to synagogue or observe Jewish rituals to any extent. Consciously, we feel pretty divorced from Judaism. How could our being Jewish have any effect upon us and our values? Such thinking confuses being Jewish with being religious —and a quite Protestant sense of being religious, at that—and it assumes that Jewish values are transmitted by formal religious activities like services, ceremonies and instruction. In part that is true, but only partly so. We have been so taken with our propaganda that Judaism is one of America's three great religions— Protestantism, Catholicism and, small but equal, Judaism—that we have repressed our differences from Christianity and thus misconceived that which we share with it. Again, a historical look will be of help to us.

The thoroughgoing identification of being Jewish with being religious, and being religious with the Christian sense of belonging to a church, was born with the Emancipation. In the Roman Empire Jews were considered nationals of the province of Judea, albeit with strange religious beliefs they fanatically upheld. The very term "Jew," which derives from this Roman usage, is not strictly religious as, say, Mosaist or Sinaiist or Covenanter would be. And in the Middle Ages, with Jews segregated, the sense of their separate peoplehood easily maintained itself within and without the ghetto. The modern, secular state changed that notion of Jewishness, at least formally, when it divorced religion and nationality, making the former, including Christianity, a far more private, personal activity than it had been.

Thus, when the leaders of the various Western European states considered giving Jews the rights of citizenship, they wanted to be certain that their Jewishness would not undermine their loyalty to the state. Napoleon went so far as to ask the leaders of French Jewry a dozen specific questions. To be understood and accepted, the French Jewish spokesmen explained their community in the terms of the prevailing culture: Jewishness was simply another religion. By defining their Jewish identity in private, as distinct, say, from ethnic or national terms, they assured their organized status and justified their right to citizenship. Emancipated Jewries everywhere have followed that line—which is why anti-Zionists have always worried about the charge of dual loyalty. The effect of such reasoning as it filtered down into the community has been to give Jews, particularly those who lived in largely non-Jewish areas, the impression that the Jews were essentially only another church. We shall never understand our ties to our Jewishness until we straighten out this misconception.

Christianity, early in its history, created the social structure called "church." For its religious purposes a group brought together in terms of common belief and staying together for common celebration seemed the proper social form. To this day, to be a Christian means to join the church, though Christian groups differ as to where the true church is to be found.

The sociology of religion shows that the Christian social pattern is quite unusual. The Buddhists, for example, are in part organized on a creedal base, but the fundamental social entity of Buddhist life is the sangha, the order of monks. They are the center of the life of the faithful. In many Buddhist groups a young man will, in preadolescence, be taken to a Buddhist monastery to spend at least one night. He has thus, symbolically, become a member of the order, even though the rest of his life may be spent as a normal, married businessman in the community. He will maintain his contact with the sangha through respect for the monks and their teaching, through giving them the alms by which they live and through the various shrines and ceremonies he attends. In contrast with Roman Catholicism, Buddhist religious life pivots about the monastic order and its activities. Hence, laymen are as a result somewhat more at the periphery.

For Moslems, on the other hand, the sense of corporate self, the Umma, the people or nation, is far more inclusive than it is for Christians. Islam is not the religious element within society. Augustine's notion of two cities and Luther's concept of the two powers lend themselves to social distinctions—between religion and power, or between religion and culture—which are foreign to Moslem belief. Rather, in Islam, culture and state and religion completely interpenetrate in a way that goes far beyond the medieval Christian efforts to turn Europe into Christendom. The special corporate form that Islam takes is a vital part of the unique faith taught by Mohammed.

The Jews too have a characteristic social form, and it likewise stemmed from their understanding of their destiny. To insist that because today the Jews live largely among Christians they must see themselves in Christian terms is not realism but self-hate. Democratic pluralism permits and morality demands that they think of themselves in their own and not someone else's terms. The Jews are obviously not a church, for they are not essentially united by doctrines, sacraments, hierarchy, or other signs of a church. Not even in the classic eras of supposed Jewish orthodoxy could the Pharisees or the medieval Jewish philosophers agree on what the necessary beliefs of Jewish faith are. While men perform the commandments, God is never understood in Judaism as a direct participant in them, so that through such acts, men are touched with His almighty power. And the only hierarchy Jews acknowledge is that of learning and piety. In fact, there is no Biblical word we can easily translate as church. *Synagogue,* our modern word for our local religious buildings is taken from the Greek, and means "place to gather together."

The Bible, however, does not hesitate to give terms for the Jews. Again and again it calls them *am,* "a people," and sometimes *goi,* "a nation." But it will help us, I think, to avoid both terms for the moment. In the American environment, with its homogenized citizenry, the term "people" seems to mean only individuals. And "nation" is too closely connected with state or government today to apply to world Jewry. Rather I suggest we use the sociologist's label, "ethnic group." Its Greek root, *ethnos,* was used as an early translation for "nation" in the Bible, though not until Roman times was it applied to the Jews themselves. In modern sociological usage the term includes the various characteristics that we associate with the Jewish group.

We can see this clearly in the early Hebrews. Like the other communities with whom they came in contact in the ancient Near East—the Perizzites, the Girgashites, the Hittites, the Hivites—the Hebrews probably had some original genealogical bond. However, they are more easily recognized as united by a common language or dialect, a unified area of settlement, a sense of their history, a living tradition; in short, they have a distinct culture. Such a group is hardly a church. It was once called an *ethnos,* and because such groups still exist we describe them as *ethnic.* The Jews begin as such an ordinary ethnic group.

What changed the simple ethnos, the Hebrews, into the people of Israel was finding Adonai, God, and covenanting themselves to Him. From a Christian perspective this should have turned the Hebrew folk into a church. It did not work that way then or since. Though the Jews transformed their simple culture into a profound and complex Covenant with God, they never gave up their essentially ethnic character. Thus, the absence of dogma in Judaism is but another sign that the Jews continued to maintain themselves as a people and not as a church. Maimonides, for all his authority in medieval Judaism, was in his daily life a practicing physician, not a religious official of formal hierarchical status. He did author a Jewish creed of thirteen principles which, according to his philosophy, every Jew should profess. His contemporaries and successors, notably Hasdai Crescas and Joseph Albo, found Maimonides' formulation unacceptable. The result was that Maimonides' creed came into Jewish practice only in the form of the hymns, *Yigdal* (where the thirteen assertions are easily identified) and *Adon Olam* (where they have been condensed), and as a meditation. Such statements of belief may be useful to a Jew, but they are not necessary, for belonging to the Jewish ethnos is prior to any particular statement of Jewish belief.

What primarily binds Jews to one another over the centuries is ethnic ties. Hebrew, their common language, always made possible international Jewish communication, though some communities were not expert in it. A church does not need a language, Protestants would assert, and the role of Latin in Catholicism—which once managed to survive the anomaly of not being New Testament Greek—is now in serious decline. But one cannot compare the place of Latin in Roman Catholicism even at its height to the use of Hebrew among Jews in the past and certainly not today. Latin was always an institutional language limited to an elite. But every Jew studied Hebrew, an ignorant man being one who only knew a little of the Torah. Thus, when Hebrew was displaced by other languages, it never was absent from the life of the folk. Indeed, scholars have argued that the Jews created other Jewish languages—Yiddish and Ladino among the living, and a half-dozen or more among the dead—to keep Hebrew alive amidst the German or Spanish they spoke every day. And the very production of so secular a thing as a language itself testifies to the potency of Jewish ethnicity.

A church can well manage without a land of its own. Vatican City is more an anachronism than a real state, a big churchyard rather than a significant polity. By contrast, love of the Land of Israel and devotion to Jerusalem run deeply and steadily throughout Jewish history. The very calendar is geared to it. Pesach, Shavuot and Sukkot, the major seasonal festivals, correspond to the Israeli agricultural cycle. Jews on the other side of the equator have their seasons reversed. It makes no difference in their practice. In Buenos Aires and Melbourne, Pesach is celebrated in what is locally autumn and Sukkot comes in the spring. From early medieval times Jewish settlements south of the equator have continued to celebrate the Jewish festivals in terms of the seasons of the Land of Israel.

The examples could be expanded indefinitely to show that Jewish life is, by Christian standards, more ethnic than religious. Jewish jokes are not only about rabbis and God. Jewish cooking is not substantially connected with the limits set by *kashrut*. Jewish music is far more extensive than liturgical chant and prayer settings. Jewish poetry speaks of topics that have no place in the prayerbook. The Jewish consciousness has few doctrinal inhibitions, embracing Marx, Freud and Einstein, plus many others equally nonobservant. And the Gentiles likewise have not distinguished between the skeptics and the pious in meting out Jewish martyrdom. The members of an ethnos share its destiny though they may not care for this or that ideology current within it. So, while victims of the Holocaust may not all have lived as Jews, they all died as Jews. In happy contrast, the atheistic Israeli is without any question my Jewish brother. For a "religion," such characteristics would be anomalous. For the Jews they are normal.

Consider the odd alternatives by which one becomes a Jew.

Normally one is born Jewish, and that settles the issue of identity. True, boys are circumcised, but if the doctors rule circumcision would endanger a child's life his circumcision is delayed or dispensed with, without any question as to his Jewishness. A male child who dies without circumcision is fully a Jewish child. Girls require no ceremony of any kind—and it is through the mother that one's Jewish identity, as a matter of birth, is established!

A church requires baptism for membership, in some cases delayed until the child has reached the age of consent and can personally accept the faith which characterizes his church. Ethnic groups operate differently. A Turk is one born into a Turkish family and an Eskimo has Eskimo descent. Jews share that ethnic sense of identity. Yet, because Jewish ethnicity is complex, in the exceptional case, one becomes a Jew by will and deed, by conversion. Thus, Jewishness can also come in the normal religious way. So we accept it as proper for Sammy Davis, Jr., and his then bride-to-be, Mai Britt, to embrace Judaism. Yet by Jewish teaching, their children were as a matter of birth Jewish. What was decision in one generation is biology in the next. Ethnicity goes that far in Judaism.

The pattern is already Biblical, as the rabbis taught. When Ruth, the good woman from the hated Moabite people, wishes to become a Jewess, she does it by simple declaration, "Thy people shall be my people and thy God my God." She accepts Jewish ethnicity as well as the Covenant. The reverse case, a Jew who converts to another faith, is governed by the same ethnic sense. As Jewish law sees it, despite his new beliefs, he cannot stop being a Jew. He cannot forfeit what is his by birth. He may lose certain privileges and become liable to certain penalties, but if he wishes to return he need not convert to Judaism. A sign of serious intent is generally all that is required. The accepted rule is that a Jew who sins is nonetheless a Jew—which should be quite comforting to most of us.

The Jews are neither a church nor a nationality, but a strange mixture of both. We are an ethnos, though not an ordinary one, for we have an unusual ethos. We are a folk distinguished historically by its faith, a people transformed by its religion.

We have difficulty defining ourselves to the world, because there are so few examples of our peculiar sort of hybrid. Perhaps the group closest in social form to the Jews are the Sikhs of India, best known for the fact that their men, despite their modern dress, always wear a turban. They too are a distinct ethnic group with what anthropologists call a "high religion." (Among primitive peoples with local gods, the mixture of ethnicity and religion is standard. A universal God, however, is rarely linked to a specific folk.) Unlike the Jews the Sikhs have remained settled on their native soil since the foundation of their separate faith about the beginning of the sixteenth century. Though there is a strong universal concern in their religion, they have not had much impact upon the general movement of civilization in India or the West. The history of religion provides some other examples of a faith with an ethnic base. Nonetheless there are so few of them that no term has been coined to describe this social structure.

The ethnic aspect of Jewishness should be differentiated from that of an American ethnic church, say the German or the Swedish Lutheran. Such churches are different from others of their denomination by virtue of the folk ties among the members. Sermons or prayers may still be given in the language of the old country, native costumes and foods may come out for certain occasions, the social style of the membership may still be quite homeland-oriented. Nonetheless, the ethnic activities are essentially extrinsic to the religion. The grandchildren of the immigrants may no longer be consciously German or Swedish, but they may still be fully Lutheran. The ministry may mourn the passage of the old-timers and their special devotion to the faith. But it will not be able to argue on Christian grounds that loyalty to the church is being compromised when one insists on the exclusive use of English and the abolition of the pre-Lenten *smor-*

*gasbord.* In contrast, Jewish religiosity and Jewish ethnicity are inseparable. Those Reform Jews who have tried to eliminate the ethnic side of their Judaism have regularly ended up leaving their erstwhile coreligionists for Ethical Culture, Unitarianism, or some other non-Jewish universalism. In one notorious case, Solomon Schindler, a rabbi of Temple Israel, Boston, left his pulpit to found a creedless, community church.

When we inquire, then, how Jewishness makes itself felt in the lives of Jews, we must understand that we are not talking about the activities of a church but of the diverse, encompassing, multilevel effects that an ethnic group has upon its members. That is to say, folkways, understood in a very broad sense, are the primary medium for transmitting the Jewish ethos, at whose heart has been the Jewish ethical passion. No better educational strategy is known to us. Values are always transmitted with more lasting effect through life than through study or preaching. When we are young, the people we see around us and the ideas we hear about us become the models about which we shape our lives. Long before psychoanalysts spoke of introjection, ethnic groups shaped character less by formal, religious instrumentalities than by informal, apparently "secular" ones. For all the Jewish emphasis on the great religious institutions, the school and the synagogue, they were expected only to extend a process carried out by home and community, not to begin it or substitute for it.

The Jewish strategy for forming human beings is founded on the family, which, over the generations, has provided not merely shelter and nurture, but motivation and standards as well. It was not through orientation courses for the about-to-be-married or "how-to" manuals for young parents that the Jewish people succeeded at this. The values were transmitted as a natural part of growing up and maturing. One's parents and grandparents got married to stay married. Divorces were available, since people can be intolerable, but one could see that marriage was entered not on a trial basis, but in hopes of working out one's humanity there. So, too, Jewish males learned from childhood that fidelity and worthy progeny are more important than sexual prowess and variety, while Jewish females grew up seeing that creating a warm but demanding home life is more significant than finding eternal romance or maintaining unfading youth. In this ethos, parenthood is not incidental, but, for all its burdens, is the most important responsibility of one's existence. To create a good family is here a vocation; to raise good children the single most important means of personal fulfillment.

The hidden truth behind all the novelistic complaints about the Jewish mother is the ethnic passion for child-shaping. The parents and grandparents cannot wait for the child to be born, and then they devote themselves with gusto to making him or her a proper person. The Yiddish put the elusive goal of Jewish character training into two highly charged phrases. When a child was bad, he was told not to be a *vilde chayeh*—literally, a "wild beast"—or, more positively, that he should be a *mentsch*—literally, but lamely, a "person." For all that those terms leave much un-clarified, they carried tremendous power. The parents invested their lives in them, and the child learned, without ever being ex-plicitly told, that life has to do with character and standards, that it begins between husband and wife and then moves on to what happens between parent and child.

They did not speak much Yiddish in Alex Portnoy's home, yet if only from his fabulously inflated pathology, we know that the same ethnic shaping process was at work on him. Philip Roth makes it clear that, for all the trauma she induces, Sophie Portnoy created Alex's conscience. And made it strong enough so that, for all his sexual bravado, Alex knows that he is sick, knows that he may not simply give in to his cravings, and knows that he must work to cure them. In a society as unhealthy as ours, Alex, I suggest, can lay claim to moral stature. What is more, though his job, Assistant Commissioner of Human Rights of the City of New York, may be part of the black humor of the book, like the rest it carries moral freight. There is no hint that

Alex does not like his thankless job or that his neurosis makes it impossible for him to function in the service of the downtrodden. His conscience was shaped with that much staying power. Roth did not name his mother Sophie ("Wisdom") for nothing. Alex's formal Jewish education was a fiasco. But because Jewishness is largely a matter of being part of an ethnos, it had some creative effect on him anyway.

Think for a moment of the way in which your own family experience carried forward—in a modern way, to be sure—the old Jewish sense of a good life. For many people it is most easily recovered in associations with food. All the jokes about chicken soup are a testimony to the unique importance of food to the Jewish family, to its special emphasis on feeding and eating. Chicken soup declares the importance of life and the duty to accept and live it. The obverse appears in the attitude toward medicine and doctors. Sickness must be defeated, so physicians have priestly, saving powers. With the overcoming of illness a major responsibility, hypochondria can become a common defense against burdens, and taking pills has almost ritual significance. Both patterns have had to adapt themselves to changes in nutrition and health care. But it is a tribute to ethnic resilience that Jewish cocktail parties always have a disproportionate amount of food to liquor as compared with Gentile ones, and every new therapy, from diets of poly-unsaturated fats to primal screaming, quickly attracts a disproportionate number of Jews seeking life.

I could expand on the directions in which you might let your memory wander seeking the power of Jewish ethnicity at work in your own childhood. I will limit myself to one more suggestion, because I want to make clear that I do not see ethnicity, for all its benefits, as without problems. I want to show how, even in what seems a negative aspect of Jewish ethnicity, something of the positive Jewish attitude toward life emerges. Jews of the past generation or so have been widely criticized by their renegades and leaders alike for their materialism—in itself a sign of the standards the group is expected to share. The roots of the materialism, I think, are not hidden. Most American Jews are descended from families who had for several centuries been deprived, to put it mildly. The migration of Jews to the United States, a land widely rumored in Eastern Europe to be impure and sinful, was powered by hunger and the desire for personal security. Hence when the Depression gave way to the post-World War II economic boom in which Jews shared, all the hopes created by years of underprivilege poured forth in a flood of acquisition and consumption.

Children growing up in a contemporary Jewish family cannot fail to be impressed by the material concern that is so much a part of the family life. In some families it will go to the extent of destroying whatever spirit the children have. I have great appreciation, therefore, for the youthful rebellion that takes the form of voluntary poverty in dress, travel or living arrangements. With parents who are so things-giving and goods-oriented, the most effective form of rebellion is the contemporary mendicancy of blue jeans and knapsack.

My real concern, however, is to point out how, amidst this negative thrust in the Jewish ethos, the positive makes itself felt. That is, most Jewish materialism is lavished on enhancing the marriage, the home and the family. Thus, Jewish husbands are statistically more likely than non-Jews to desert rather than divorce their wives. The reason seems to be that they want to be married, not divorced, but marriage means providing for wife and children in a way they feel inadequate to. So, the family money quarrels are likely to be over furnishings and clothes and children's needs, all with the overtones of what befits a Jewish family and what is expected in the Jewish community—all going back, in effect, to the two-thousand-year-old Jewish marriage contract, the *ketubah,* and its clause "I will cherish, honor, support and maintain thee according to the custom of Jewish husbands." Even amidst the materialism and despite its deleterious effects, I am arguing, the positive side of the Jewish ethos makes itself felt.

Of course, other families in the United States and other ethnic groups show some of the same concerns and patterns. I do not think there is something totally different about Jewish life that can be isolated as *the* Jewish factor in existence. Rather, since Jews—except for the Hasidim—do not live in cultural segregation, their lives are overwhelmingly like those of most other Americans. What concerns us here, particularly since we can no longer put our confidence in the beneficial drift of the general culture, is how, amidst the great similarities between Jewish and Gentile life, the continuing positive Jewish differences arise. Were Jews still devout, we could answer that their religion skews their statistics in the general patterns. But we are not devout, and I am arguing that our Jewishness is functioning primarily on another level, the ethnic one. The Jewish family thus gives the lives of its children a permanent cast. The personal directions they then choose will vary. But from growing up in a Jewish family one has already integrated certain social traits with those of his individuality.

The socialization begun in the family is substantially reinforced by living in a Jewish community. Two aspects are worthy of note. First, there are the strong ties to the various branches of one's own family. Jews may not have dogmas, but they do have relatives! Leaving them out of a *bar mitzvah* or a wedding is the Jewish equivalent of heresy. Somehow, we are accountable to uncles and cousins even as we are to parents. Though we do not visit much, we shall hear about one another, and at the events when the clan gathers—a circumcision, a new home, a funeral—we shall quickly, and sometimes openly, evaluate one another. Quite early we get a sense that we owe something to our relatives, and later, despite class and culture differences which may arise, we still have a special responsibility to one another.

This feel for the greater family is common to a number of ethnic groups—the Italians and Chinese, for example—though it tends to be expressed in somewhat different ways. The Jewish sense of family, however, is further differentiated by the way in which it reaches out to all other Jews—with lessening intensity, to be sure. Perhaps it begins with something apparently as neutral as a choice of housing. Jewish families still care to live near other Jews, and Jewish children will early learn which neighbors are and which are not Jewish, and, though their home is empty of prejudice, that the distinction between Jew and non-Jew is significant. In Gentile neighborhoods the family will make an effort to arrange some Jewish contacts for the child. They want the effect of a Jewish peer group. Youthful though such a group is, it is an effective model of the larger, older Jewish community, complete with its legislative and judicial powers. The parents will themselves be concerned to identify who among newcomers in the area or among notables in the news is Jewish. They will, without explicit instruction—for, though all utilize it, who knows how it works?—train their child to develop that special ethnic "radar" by which one Jew recognizes another despite his similarity to all other Americans.

The most efficient instrument by which this sense of community and values is transmitted, made all the more effective by its being casual and unplanned, is gossip. Jews regularly talk about other Jews, and the children hear. A good deal of such talk is more opinion than fact. If James Levine is the new young sensation as a director at the Metropolitan Opera and Dr. Judah Folkman, a rabbi's son, discovers a key link in the growth of cancer cells, that is good for the Jews. If Abe Fortas is forced to resign from the Supreme Court because he may have behaved with impropriety and if Meir Lansky takes refuge in the State of Israel when the United States government is trying to investigate his links to organized crime, that is bad for the Jews.

Most gossip is more neighborly and less worldly, yet it is no less effective in showing our true values. So, each Jew understands that he himself is known and judged by other Jews. The greater his fame, the greater the circle of Jews who feel a share in him. In his triumphs, the community will rejoice. In his transgressions, they will all lament and suffer. In classic Judaism that was the doctrine of *kiddush* and *chilul hashem*—that is, Jewish righteousness sanctifies God's name among men, Jewish sinfulness profanes it. The older theological overtones have disappeared. The pervasive sense that acts count, not only personally, but to the community as well, has not. A modern Jew may insist he is an individual and work to free himself of the moral kinship. But it often still works as a powerful force in shaping his character.

If this were a sociological treatise we would elaborate the ways in which the individual Jew's life is touched by the Jewish community outside his home. Through formal agency and activity, there are many. Permit me to limit myself to the dramatic. These community ties come most powerfully to the surface when a community of Jews is attacked, whether in our own country or abroad. The breadth and passion of American Jewry's response to the Six-Day War was beyond anything one expected. The ethnic ties were simply much stronger than anyone had believed. Since then small crises have come and gone with varying impact on American Jewry. The surfacing of extremist black anti-Semitism, the Forest Hills housing project, the treatment of Jewish prisoners in Iraq and Syria, the momentary panic among Chilean Jews at the succession of Allende, all have tended to affect relatively few in American Jewry, mainly those with special interests. Yet the continuing struggle to free Soviet Jewry has for several years involved large numbers, and in the Nixon-McGovern campaign it became clear that a possible threat to the State of Israel could become a significant factor in the established voting patterns of American Jews. These large-scale issues not only illustrate our ethnic loyalties but also, as we do something about them, teach us anew what Jews are a people for.

Perhaps the reason Jewish ethnicity can have an effect on us in the mass as it does personally is that our people is very much like one huge family. It shows the same fierce reactions of love and hate that one has with one's immediate relatives. It comes to us with that same given-ness, that same inescapable quality, that one has with family. And it has that same sort of power over our feeling for our worth and our accomplishment that our parents have. We should, I think, take the term "children of Israel" far more literally than we do. It means Jacob's family. In many ways, despite the increase in numbers and the passage of time, that is what we remain. We are not very loyal to the family and not as concerned about them as we should be. Nonetheless the ties remain and so, too, some sense of obligation.

These apparently secular entities, the family and the community, are effective largely because they have centuries of Jewish practice behind them. The present social order may be substantially different from what Jews were once accustomed to. Nonetheless, many of the values that family and community transmit remain valid, though transformed to meet the new social situation. The old passion for learning is fulfilled largely through the university rather than the yeshivah, and the traditional emphasis on charity is carried out as much by supporting governmental welfare programs as by giving to private and Jewish institutions. The major change is in the form; the human substance seems largely the same.

We have not had to refer in this discussion to school and synagogue, to religious law and custom, to see how Jewishness produces Jews. Though I consider the description I have given rather artificial, I specifically omitted the religious factor from consideration in order to clarify how being part of an ethnos itself affects individual character.

When the home is also religious, when children and parents are involved in Jewish study and communal Jewish observance, the work of the ethnos is vigorously reinforced and refined. What is largely subliminal in folkways becomes articulated and analyzed in a tradition, particularly where it is as verbal and intellectual as the Jewish tradition. I do not think it altogether possible to express in language what fills the Jewish self. But that is just why the classic sayings and poems and rites, for all that they are but fragments of the truth, are supremely valuable. They say much of what can be said and show us how to do some of what can be done. Thus, through them we come to link mind and heart consciously to what was until then simple custom or un- reflective pattern. But even without this broad superstructure of Jewish tradition that so many Jews unfortunately lack, Jewish ethnicity, I am saying, has already worked to influence their lives.

Ethnicity accomplishes another purpose central to the Jewish ethos: persistence through time. The Jewish people has, from Biblical days on, understood its purpose in history to be making the whole world just, compassionate and peaceful. Millenniums have passed since the Jews pledged themselves to this task, yet we have not given up our hope that it will one day become real- ity. At the same time, what we have undergone has taught us that it is not likely to come to pass speedily, though we pray it will. As one rabbinic tradition puts it, if you are planting a tree when they tell you the Messiah has come, first finish planting the tree and then go see. So an essential part of Jewish dedication is the will to last out history and its vicissitudes. With such an un- common goal, the Jews organized themselves in an equally un- common way. The Jews are an ethnos and have remained one, I contend, because that social form best fits their function of faithful survival.

Just when Jewish ethnicity became so integral to the Biblical view of man and history is impossible to say. Religious tradition- alists would insist that it is apparent at the very inception of Jew- ishness. When Abraham was called into Covenant with God, he was promised that he would be the father of a populous nation living in the Land of Canaan. The full people was then brought into conscious being at the Exodus to go to Sinai to receive the Torah. They were preserved in their long trek through the wil- derness and brought into their promised land so they might ob- serve this law. In this view, Judaism has not known a split, ever, between the folk and this faith, between ethnic form and messianic purpose. From the beginning, God knew what He was doing.

Religious liberals would interpret this connection between ethnicity and spiritual endurance as a product of human growth. As the people of Israel came to understand its God and its responsibility to Him, it fashioned itself, sometimes consciously, sometimes unconsciously, into a folk whose life, from prophetic rebuke to kings to rabbinic law that regulated markets and employment, reflected the justice and mercy that it felt its God demanded. In the Babylonian exile of the sixth century B.C.E., the people learned their ethnicity depended more on the presence of their God than on residence on their land. In the subsequent centuries of resettlement the ethnic side of their Jewishness was renewed, but not to the point of having their own king.

Yet, in this same period the religious reforms of Ezra—an insistence upon the Hebrew language and a prohibition of intermarriage—strengthened Jewish ethnicity. By Roman times ethnicity and religion were indissoluble. The Romans considered these peculiar people nationals of the province Judea, yet, equally, adherents of an odd faith, most obstinately upheld. The Jews too thought of themselves in terms of both their peoplehood and their religion, though they perceived no distinction between them. In these centuries, then, the classic form of Jewishness came to be. Some social forms the Jews had not found essential to their existence: living on the land, monarchy and political autonomy. Existence as an ethnos, albeit without these normal signs of an ethnos, apparently could not be sacrificed. So the Jews became the strange ethnoreligious hybrid that we still find them to be.

Now let us see how ethnicity operates to achieve its historic purposes. Ethnicity creates multiple bonds of loyalty, which reinforce the power of the Jewish moral dream and are a strong armor against the blows of history. As Freud showed, men are not kindly disposed to those who wish to make them moral. The resentment is not decreased because one acknowledges that the standards being urged are right. No one loves his alarm clock. Were men not so resistant to goodness, there would be no need for the Jewish people in history. But, men being as willful as they are, being a Jew among them cannot be easy.

Were, then, the Jews only a free association of the like-minded, a club for intellectuals, a temporary gathering of those with similar sentiments, they could never have taken what history has thrown at them; they would long since have given up their gorgeous but mad vision. A church is far more durable than most voluntary associations, for it reinforces intellect with personal devotion, ritual, tradition and hierarchy. But the Jews have been few, scattered and despised. If one of their primary concerns is to preserve in purity a purpose which might easily be lost in compromise or accommodation, then its group needs an inner unity far more compact than creed and sacrament and ministry could supply. The Jews are an ethnos because in that way land and language and lore and literature and folkways, all work to make Jewish commitment adequate to the task of outlasting history so as to transform it.

Perhaps the chief example of the historic power of Jewish ethnicity is how the Jews turned the ghetto experience into a richly human way of life. In the segregated community every aspect of existence from dress to philosophy was permeated with a distinctive, formative Jewish style. Because it knew itself to be an unusual ethnos, it could not only survive the ghetto but live there with nobility.

Today that shaping ethnicity is far less visible, and where it is most evident it is often most heartily decried. The complaint is common that contemporary Jews are too thoroughly secular, that their Jewishness is too much lox and bagels rather than Covenant and commandment. It would be difficult to deny that most of us prefer Jewish association to Jewish dedication. The call for more serious Jewishness awakens great sympathy in me, but anyone who does not appreciate the indispensable service

Jewish ethnicity renders Judaism does not understand either our era or the special nature of being Jewish.

Ours is a time of widespread agnosticism, at least on the surface. Most people cannot see themselves as in any way significantly believing. If we insist that to be a Jew means one must be "spiritual," we will be not only historically inaccurate but irrelevant to most modern Jews. In such a time as this the virtue of Jews' having strong ethnic ties proves itself. Ethnicity now furnishes the reserve staying power for the community. For, though we may not be very "spiritual," most American Jews are still somehow quite Jewish. And being Jewish through their eating, drinking, joking, social style, companionship, they cannot easily shake the old dream. God lurks behind the chopped liver. The caterer, for all the vulgarity he may have fostered, must be seen as a low-level, latter-day Levite, serving the ritual assemblies of the Jewish masses, the commonalty that is the Jewish people.

Being an ethnos keeps us from chucking the commitments of millenniums in one deviant decade or two. Even if American-Jewish life is sick and perhaps dying, as is surely possible, we shall at least linger for a while. Ethnicity has bound us too tightly to slip away from our identity quickly. And that gives us some generations in which the Jewish soul can reassert itself and create a communal base on which to rebuild our way of life.

One might call this holding action the defensive social function of ethnicity. But ethnicity also provides a positive thrust to Jewish faithfulness. Being a people among other peoples of the world, the Jews cannot readily withdraw from history. Their perspective is not fixed on one aspect of life called "the religious." Being a people, the Jews are subjected to the full social effects of time and change and circumstance. Until the Emancipation their world view was conditioned by their segregated existence, and their social responsibility was restricted largely to their own communities. Since the Emancipation, the duties of the Jewish community vis-à-vis the Jews have greatly constricted, except in the State of Israel, where they have greatly expanded. Yet even today in the Diaspora, being a people involves Jews in activities far more diverse than those of a church and has provided the model for sending Jews out of their community to work for the benefit of mankind, not only in "spiritual" matters but in all those areas where the real problems of man are met.

The contemporary Christian puzzlement over the relationship of the secular to the religious finds little echo in Judaism. The faiths may claim the same God, but their diverse senses of His service are reflected in their diverse institutional forms. When one can think that religion is centered in the church and its activity, it is easy to believe that the rest of life is secular. In Judaism the ethnos, with all the secular overtones of that term retained, is the bearer of the Jewish ideal. The synagogue is only one place, though an important one, where the Jew lives out his Jewishness. But Jewish law and teaching reach far beyond liturgy and personal piety, into such secular realms as rents and damages, baths and clothing.

Out of their secular heritage stripped of most of its Jewish religious character, modern Jews created the State of Israel. There the Jews have done what the Bible tells the people of Israel to do, to build a community on their own land and become a nation, though a special one, among the nations. For a church to establish a state would be quite odd. But not for the Jews. In a state there is no hope of separating preachment from practice, for a state is immersed in every nasty social problem. And to be a Jewish state means to stand precisely at the junction of Biblical ideals and political necessities.

The frighteningly high moral demands made on the State of Israel arise from this unique ethicopolitical position. Idealistic talk about this nation's special role as "a light unto the nations" comes easily in the pulpit or the living room. Running a small, imperiled, developing country is tough and complicated. The need to survive subordinates every other need, and ethics then may seem an indulgence. Yet, if the State of Israel manifested merely the same viciousness as every other modern estate, then I—and most Israelis, I am certain—would feel this behavior to be a betrayal of the Jewish people and its tradition. How can a country whose major history text is the Bible avoid the prophetic teaching that politics is a means and not an end?

Most Diaspora Jews are proud of the State of Israel for what it has done to transform the normal dictates of politics to a more humane style of using power. In a most difficult situation, one where the only realistic possibility is often to do a lesser evil, again and again the Israelis have made a continuing, exceptional effort to behave decently. In rescuing the poor and unwanted, in uniting its diverse social classes and immigrant peoples, in trying to deal constructively with Arabs within its borders, in limiting reprisals against neighbor states for their attacks upon unarmed civilians, in creating an army which must win without brutalizing its soldiers or militarizing the population, the State of Israel has provided an utterly uncommon example of dealing with difficult and ugly realities without moral capitulation. Thus, in the midst of the crisis produced by Russia's rearming of Egypt after the Six-Day War, the Israelis changed their law on education. The State had previously undertaken to supply free education for all children through grade 8, but the upper limit was now raised to grade 10. In other words, the Israelis refused to sacrifice the future of their children to the growing cost of jet fighters.

I make no claim that Israeli politics are pure or, if not pure, beyond criticism because of the imperatives of survival. Israeli indignation at controversial government decisions indicates what nonsense that is. Otherworldliness is suitable only for another world. The State of Israel is quite definitely part of our sinful, ambiguous history, for it is just there that the ethicization of mankind must ultimately take place.

What is as astonishing as it is revelatory is the standard by which the critics of the State of Israel make their judgments against it. They allow it no errors, no lapses, no human frailties.

Actions they might be willing to overlook in other governments, men and power being what they are, are blown up here to major character defects. They refuse to use comparative standards and see what other nations in a similar situation might do or what, in fact, the surrounding peoples take for granted. Where the State of Israel is concerned, the moral standards are absolute and no deviation is permitted. Perhaps this demand is an inevitable reaction to years of Jewish propaganda about the glorious achievements of the State of Israel. But it is also based on the assumption that the Jewish people cannot simply be a people like all other peoples, that it must, under any circumstances, be a people of ethics par excellence.

Jewish radicals insist they are denouncing the State of Israel on purely universal, humanitarian—that is, Marxist—grounds. But why do they demand of Israel what they would never expect of Cuba or Chile or Tanzania? Though they claim no tie with the Jewish people, they still hold fast to its chosenness. From Jews they expect more, and they tell you so with vehemence. Apparently, despite the effort to think in global terms, one still gets more hysterical when one's own family is involved.

The Israelis may not have done all they might have done to raise the economic level of Sephardic immigrants, to open up their establishment to other than old East Europeans and their families, to protect the rights of the Arabs and Bedouin whose lands they have held since 1967. Despite the claims of some Jewish mystics and right-wing enthusiasts, the State of Israel is obviously not the *athalta d'g'ula,* the beginning of the messianic redemption. It is a good start at the humane use of political power. I cannot think of another state that has done nearly as well in as difficult a position. And I do not see that it could have happened were not Jewish ethnicity so potent a moralizing instrument.

Ethnicity can, of course, be abused and then ethnocentrism displaces ethics in the Jewish ethos. In the immigrant American-Jewish community, years of persecution made themselves felt in a world view that knew two hostile camps, Jews and *goyim,* with the former always right. Today, with the memories of the Holocaust so real and the sense of isolation in 1967 still painful, there is every temptation, when social tensions run high, for Jews to think that their only duty is to defend their own community, in Forest Hills or Israel. So, in the McGovern-Nixon campaign it was widely suggested in the Jewish community that while Jews would normally think a Democrat best for the United States, in this case the Republican, Nixon, was good for the State of Israel. The possibility that the Jews might place ethnic self-interest above the people's moral responsibility was considered even in the days of the prophets, and from Amos on, they condemned it. God's Covenant with Israel would never excuse corporate Jewish unrighteousness. And the people of Israel accepted this teaching and recognized this judgment against them as revelation. From those days to these, ethnocentrism has been more a Jewish response to persecution than a commitment demanded by the Jewish ethos. What should surprise us is not that it still arises in overreaction to our enemies, but how steadily Jewish ethnicity has pointed toward a universal goal, when during much of human history it was the means that enabled this people to survive.

I am saying that Jewish ethnicity, for all its potential for misuse, is an incomparably valuable instrument for social morality. I am suggesting that even when this people has been ailing, its special sort of ethnicity has enabled it to endure long enough for a sensitive minority to arise and bring their ethnic brothers back to Jewish vitality. Two great Holocaust-like events dismayed Jewry some centuries ago, the Expulsion from Spain at the end of the fifteenth century and the Chmielnicki massacres in Poland of the mid-17th century. The former seemed to break the spirit of the great Sephardic Jewish community and physically scattered its families across the eastern Mediterranean countries. Only in due course to give rise to the Lurianic Kabbalah which, by the seventeenth century, animated the communities of world Jewry. So, too, Chmielnicki and his Cossacks devastated the heartland of Ashkenazic Jewry, leaving behind them what contemporary observers called quite self-consciously a "black despair." Only in due course to give rise to the Hasidic movement, which refreshed Jewish existence in a way that now, after Hitler's Holocaust, still evokes our admiration.

I am claiming that, despite greater temptation to disappear or die out than most groups have ever had to face, this odd ethnos has learned how to persist, not only as a historic entity but as an idealistic one. I am insisting that though over the ages individual Jews—whose high sense of global responsibility I have often found admirable—have converted or drifted away from Jewishness, this people has kept alive its messianic passion and again and again has created a disproportionate number of morally determined individuals. This accomplishment was so durable, the example of our grandfathers and great-grandfathers was so potent, that we, a rather faithless generation, still manage to show their values in our lives.

What might our lives be like if, instead of passively showing what remains of our Jewishness, we consciously affirmed it and brought the power of our will and determination to our Jewish being? Just deepening one's personal roots would already differentiate one from the common condition of modern mankind. Everyone complains that our society is too big, too anonymous, that our lives are characterized by *anomie,* nonattachment, emptiness, meaninglessness. Because we change neighborhoods or classes or countries with comparative ease, we belong nowhere, and no way of life is more than another style that we have momentarily adopted. Jewish ethnicity has long since learned to overcome rootlessness. To be a Jew means to have a bond with every other Jew—and somehow know how to find him. Almost every Jew has his own amazing tale of how his ethnic radar once found him companionship in an unfamiliar place. My neighbor, who creates new computers, tells of a conference of mathematicians and physicists, where representatives of Iron Curtain countries and the West began their sessions with great tension. But that night their bull session ended with the new acquaintances discussing whether their children would still care about being Jewish.

When a Jew comes to a new community there are places for him to go, people he can quickly get to know, and even too many Jewish organizations to join. Become involved in that community—and none is not desperate for workers—and you are no longer a megalopolitan cipher. It does not take long for you to find people here who knew people you know there or are related to them. The web reaches everywhere. In an age where most ties are few and feeble, our most likely complaint about the Jewish community is that it remains too fiercely possessive of its own. But such concern is the antidote to anonymity.

Beyond people and institutions, there awaits the rich humus of Jewish culture. The Bible is the book we always meant to read, and rabbinic wisdom picks up its insights and applies them with a realism and compassion that is legendary. The philosophic-minded may ponder medieval problems with Saadia or Maimonides, or contemporary ones with Cohen and Buber. Lovers of folklore may explore the tales of Yemen or the humor and proverbs of Eastern Europe. There is poetry from Provence and Spain and folksong from the farthest reaches of Sephardic and Ashkenazic Jewry. There is modern and ancient literature, Hebrew, Yiddish and English. There is history and law, mysticism and theology, the varied products of American Jewry and of the State of Israel. And through it all there runs that passionate Jewish commitment to sanctify existence. What in another ethnic group would be only culture here becomes teaching as well.

The Jewish ethnos and the Jewish ethos remain effective realities. They give the individual Jew moral stamina, and messianic assurance. They summon us to continue the task our forebears began, and they teach us how not to despair in the face of frustration or failure. To be a Jew means to know from the experience of your people that morality is not without power, that mankind may not give up its hope of a decent world. Rather, the continued existence of this tiny, battered people testifies that men can transform ugly social realities into the basis for high moral achievement. We may fail. A community may go under. But the Jewish people will survive and carry on. The vision remains. It has not been and will not be forgotten. The Jewish people is a guarantee that it will yet be accomplished.

Jewish history is also a record of Jewish suffering. The Jewish accomplishment is measured against the pain Jews have been forced to bear. Had it been easy for the Jews to cultivate righteousness, the Jewish moral stamina today would be infinitely less. But this leads us to the question of whether we have the right to choose to continue our ethnos if it makes our children or later generations liable to Jewish suffering.

Let us be clear: there is no commandment that a Jew must suffer. The Jewish ethos does not commend misery as a way of pleasing God. We have known enough distress to realize there is no special virtue in it. When in *The Fixer* Bernard Malamud has his hero reject the pedagogy of crucifixion, he is fully in the spirit of Jewish teaching. Rather, we pray in the shortened daily prayer: "Keep us far from suffering and give us the fullness of the choice places of Thy earth." The suffering servant is essentially a Christian idea. Not until late medieval times, when Christian persecution began the destruction of Jewish communities, did Jewish interpreters seek to make a virtue of what had befallen them. Since then, the world has schooled us so well in suffering that talking about our pain has become a major form of relief from it. But this people has little record of asceticism and did not encourage self-mortification—though for some Jews complaining remains the most satisfactory way of avoiding the Evil Eye.

Choosing Jewishness does not mean asking to suffer—but we cannot know in advance what others will impose upon us. The Jewish martyrdom under Hitler, which once would have seemed to be the strongest argument against Jewish identity, has now paradoxically become a motive for reaffirming it. What would it mean, after Hitler's defeat, if the Jews en masse, gave up their Jewishness? It would, as Emil Fackenheim has pointed out, give Hitler his only lasting victory. The Jews would have done Hitler's work for him, and Hitler, dead, would have accomplished what he could not do alive. We may not understand or be able to explain why the six million had to die or how God could keep silent in the face of such a tragedy. Before the problem of extreme evil, there is an old tradition of Jewish agnosticism. We do not know. But the evil having been done, we know we may not abet it. Our people, of all peoples, must survive.

So, when any Jew today, not quite knowing what he believes, not quite sure why he chooses to remain Jewish, not quite certain of what he is getting into—nonetheless and despite everything—accepts his ethnicity and wills to stand firmly in the Jewish community, then his simple act says that the Jewish moral passion is greater even than this inexplicable human horror. Such a Jew, though he is not certain of what he stands for, knows that a Jew must be against viciousness and violence, the perversion of science and the dismemberment of society. He must be a witness against nihilism and barbarity, against apathy and despair. Those are negative reasons for reasserting our ethnic identity. They are not insignificant ones.

To accept Jewish ethnicity today means personally to testify that righteousness endures—the only demonstration Jews need to stage to proclaim that truth is to be here. Their presence speaks for them. As Leo Baeck said, for a Jew, existence is itself a *mitzvah*. I can understand a man who has suffered to the bone insisting that no one has the right, not even God, to ask more of him and of his family. But most Jews who want to slip away these days are more selfish than scarred. They likely have never suffered from anything worse than social slights. In any case, the Jewish people has made its decision. Not only is it in the thick of current history, it is determined to stay there. This makes the question of identity more pointed: Will you, who were born into this people, join it in this moral commitment, this unrelenting messianism? Or will you, by reducing its numbers and lessening its morals, sap its staying power?

Is our civilization so full of moral courage that it no longer needs a community of Jews? Or is our time instead so full of disillusionment about mankind, its insane wars, its tawdry politics, its exploitative societies, its absurd history, that nothing could be more important than that there be some people who are determined that all this must be changed and who will live by that belief, come what may? Words no longer inspire men. But the reality of a people which has walked through hell and come out crippled but undaunted might yet speak to those who can still hear. The Jewish ethnos by its unique presence says to our dispirited world that we may still hope for man and his history. Most of us never thought our lives said anything so grand. Jewish existence says nothing less. And I believe that we, beneath all the poses, stand for nothing different.

# CHAPTER 7

# Folk Without Faith

If ethnicity is the primary medium for the transmission of Jewish values, why can we not continue Jewishness on a purely secular level? Why should we not simply accept what most American Jews say about themselves, that they are not and cannot be religious, though they are happy to be Jewish? Surely, many American Jews live by this sense of Jewishness, and it commends itself by engendering a variety of positive Jewish obligations.

Despite the Jewish truth that it contains, I see this view as but another Marrano stratagem to keep us from facing our deepest Jewish commitments. For clarity's sake, I will, quite artificially, distinguish three separate approaches to American Jewish life which are, in effect, expressions of this desire for a folk without faith. Mostly one sees them commingled in any given life, but for the purpose of uncovering the full implications of our values I shall treat them independently. They are (1) the Jewishness of association; (2) the Jewishness of good deeds; and (3) the Jewishness of high culture.

There can be no doubt that many Jews remain Jewish mainly because they like being with other Jews. They are not necessarily uncomfortable in Gentile company; rather, because of their ethnic roots, they find special pleasure in associating with Jews. Playing cards or golf or the stock market with other Jews is enriched by a common vocabulary that was once explicitly verbal— as in the Yiddish terms *shlemiehl, m'tziyah, m'chullah, knocker* —and is now more diffusely recognizable in gesture, tone, thrust and parry. When even the insults come from a common heritage, the quarrels are more bearable. So Jews seek out other Jews in neighborhoods, in clubs, or at resorts. They generally find it difficult to say just why that is so, and a visit to New York's Harmonie Club or Chicago's Standard Club will not easily clarify it. Such institutions were founded by German not Yiddish speakers. Their cuisine is international, and their bars are utilized in a nearly normal American manner. The famed Catskill Borscht Belt remains more resolutely East European, but every year a few more hotels stop keeping kosher, while survival in a big way means adding nightclub acts and a golf course.

Nonetheless, Jews still seek out other Jews. Many will not try a new resort or cruise without finding out if there are likely to be some other Jews there. Once in a new situation, part of their exploratory agenda is to discover who is Jewish. Science says it is nonsense, but most Jews claim to be equipped with an interpersonal friend-or-foe-sensing device that enables them to detect the presence of another Jew, despite heavy camouflage. Once Jewish bonds are established, they will feel far more at home.

This attitude is the result of having grown up amid the threat of anti-Semitism and the defensiveness it bred. Yet it must have far more positive roots than that, for though the present generation of young people has known little other than social acceptance, it seems to have a similar propensity. Another, more ironic, example is the big-city intellectuals. Though they regularly used to spurn ethnic motivation, they also regularly demonstrated its power. The urban political and cultural cliques always were heavily Jewish. And while these great spirits consistently derided their heritage, they felt happiest among other such marginal Jews. I have seen, in a number of suburbs, circles of largely intermarried couples that I took to be constituted by a desire for Jewish association that kept them out of the non-Jewish community but did not let them feel altogether at home among the Jews.

A more positive form of Jewish loyalty is arrived at negatively, but nonetheless as a moral decision. Albert Einstein is the classic exemplar of this position. He felt that to desert the Jewish people after all it has been through was utterly ignoble. Further, since anti-Semitism is reprehensible, one remains a Jew as a personal refusal to conciliate this evil. I think this attitude is fairly widespread today among otherwise assimilated Jews. Though they do not make a point of associating with other Jews or otherwise displaying their ethnic origins, an anti-Semitic slur will draw not only their response but an acknowledgment of their own Jewishness. I shall be talking about the State of Israel in the next chapter, but I cannot leave the topic of Jewish loyalty without noting how many Jews, some otherwise unconcerned with the Jewish people, are personally aroused by the issue of Israeli destiny.

These modes of association seem to be the least complex level on which American Jewish life proceeds. They present themselves as the natural thing to do, even with something of a moral flair. Yet if what most commends Jewishness to us is its positive effect on the character of succeeding generations, this simple style of Jewish existence will hardly perpetuate it. Spending time with other Jews, for all the power of ethnicity, will not, all by itself, indefinitely transmit the satisfactions it imparts. They are founded not simply on social ease but on many shared intuitions and memories, as close as our last trip to Israel, as distant as the Exodus from Egypt. We would not have such pleasure eat-

ing out together if our great-grandfathers had not for so long
starved in Europe. We would not be so bitter about the stupidity
and malice of politicians if we had not fought so hard for our
rights in society and if we did not care what happened to
mankind.

Unless each new generation of Jewry makes at least the Jewish
past its own—but preferably the Jewish historic vision too—why
should it care about Jewish socializing? Even Jewish self-defense
will then provide little rationale for Jewish association. Though
metropolitan Jews have in the past few years been most directly
threatened by black demands, it remains clear that the security
of both groups is in the hands of the general society. While Jews
must fight vigorously for their rightful place in our social system,
their long-range future is essentially a factor of America's realistic practice of democracy. There will be no security for Jews
in America until all groups are secure in their rights and opportunities. Hence, Jewish self-defense is only partially an ethnic
matter. Rather, Jews will best serve their own interests by joining blacks and Mexican-Americans and Indians and other minority groups in their efforts to secure their rights. At the same time
they will create a community of effort that is itself a significant
step in attaining true democracy.

Most American Jews know that a Jewish golf club does not
perpetuate the Jewishness they enjoy. They couldn't care less.
They do not join it to foster Jewish survival, and they would not
try to defend it as anything more than their pleasure. But they
also do not want to face the fact that the Jewish bonds that make
it attractive to them will not long survive if all there is to hold
Jews together is locker-room gossip and card-room chitchat.

This danger is so obvious that most American Jews have had
to train themselves thoroughly not to move against it—or better,
to do only the minimum that Jewish survival would seem to en-
tail. We refuse to give up easily any Marrano stance. And here
we have the added defense that we obviously aren't self-hating

types. We aren't running away from our Jewishness at all! No, at this level we are only letting it die by attrition.

Apparently more and more Jews recognize the necessity of adding something substantive to Jewish association, if our ethnicity is to have its desired effect. For some years now, strange sounds have been heard from the Jewish Establishment. The American Jewish Committee, long devoted almost exclusively to Jewish self-defense and at one time quite concerned that Jewish exposure be kept to a minimum, has engaged staff to help its membership explore and strengthen their Jewish identity. The Council of Jewish Federations and Welfare Funds, which has always given lip service to the needs of Jewish education and culture, now speaks of making them a major priority and has, in fact, arranged to spend $2,500,000 over the next three years in creative projects suitable for local communities.

The New York Federation of Jewish Philanthropies—the only citywide Jewish charity fund in America that has not included the United Jewish Appeal for the State of Israel and other overseas needs—has long been considered by its critics a classic case of budgetary self-hate. Compared to the millions of dollars it channeled into settlement houses, clinics and welfare agencies to benefit an essentially non-Jewish clientele, the million-or-so dollars a year it gave to Jewish education, including America's largest community of impoverished Jews, seemed paltry. Now Federation too has upgraded its concern with Jewish education, and its new capital-fund drive will seek to establish a $20,000,000 foundation for special educational needs and projects.

Critics have charged that such moves to bolster Jewish education are as little as they are, and as late in coming, because they stem from organizational self-interest. Neither the Committee nor the Welfare Funds are seriously interested in transmitting the Jewish heritage. They are only frightened by a potential loss of members and donors. If Jews continue to drift from the community, where will the Jewish organizations get their support?

Such charges are harsh and ignore the fact that for many American Jews good deeds, notably charity and education, have for many years been the substance of their Jewishness. For a free and highly individualistic group, American Jews have compiled a phenomenal record of accomplishment in both areas.

The concern for charity goes back to the founding of the American Jewish community. When the first group of Jews reached this country in 1654—typically, they were displaced persons from Brazil, captured by pirates and ultimately released in New Amsterdam—they were initially refused permission to debark, for fear they would become a burden on the pioneer community. Peter Stuyvesant's mixture of prudence and anti-Semitism was finally overcome only when pressure from home forced him to accept the pledge of the new community that it would care for its own poor and infirm members. From that time to our own this pledge has been honored.

Naturally, there are many complaints about the amount and the direction of our giving, but on the whole the manner and amount of American Jewish philanthropy can be faulted only by comparison with its own idealistic standards. The sums of money given have no parallels in private benevolence anywhere, some would insist, not even in previous Jewish history, though American tax law complicates such judgments. Equally important, the money has been used in ways that have illustrated and sometimes set the standards for general social-welfare work. Thus, the concept of Community Chest drives for citywide charity was modeled on Jewish welfare-fund drives. And local Jewish agencies have almost always been in advance of those finding better ways to befriend the forgotten and the forlorn.

To associate oneself with Jewish benevolence is to make a positive personal contribution to keeping alive a noble tradition of mutual concern now strangely compromised by affluence. We still give extraordinarily, but not as we once did. Our new riches have not made us proportionately more generous, but rather more selfish and demanding. When Jews were poorer, those who had money were less self-indulgent. Today one might well argue that it is worth being Jewish if only to salvage and perpetuate the old Jewish sense of *tzedakah*, of righteousness expressed as charity.

How much more reason there is to keep alive the traditional Jewish concern with education! Without centuries of Hebrew schools and yeshivahs, the Jewish people could never have kept its ideals alive and relevant, and modern culture would have been impoverished by not having its Jewish intellectuals. All such achievement begins with the Jewish parents' anxiety over their child's education—mentioned already in the circumcision ceremony, eight days after birth—and is given specific direction in the Jewish school. Consider the Jewish heroes. We esteem Moses for obtaining the laws and placating God. David is more the psalmist than the conqueror. Jeremiah denounces kings and reliance on the Temple. Hillel teaches ethics. Akiba, who begins to study at forty, is the great systematizer of Oral Law. Maimonides is a doctor and philosopher; the Baal Shem a mystic; the Vilna Gaon a pioneering legal scholar. Only Theodor Herzl is a politician, and he wants to save Jews, not rule them.

Decry the excesses of *bar mitzvah* parties as one must, the *bar mitzvah* remains mankind's most civilized initiation rite. We do not knock out a tooth, give a boy his own rifle or take him to a whorehouse. To qualify among us he need not kill, bear pain, or break the otherwise accepted mores. Rather he must master an old alphabet and learn enough of an ancient tongue so he may read from a holy book. His manliness is associated with handwritten scrolls still studied in a spirit of reverent pleasure. He may be conscious only of the presents, but he cannot fail to be shaped by this moment. And if this ceremony is reinforced by a positive family attitude and continuing education, he is likely to see his life as another link in the precious moral chain: prophets, rabbis, philosophers, mystics, modernizers, Zionists.

The Jewish school exists to raise to the level of conscious thought and personal understanding the values that the family and community pass on almost unconsciously. While the dominant society works to condition us to its own exploitative ends, the Jewish school works to extend and strengthen the ethical values of home and community that can enable us to resist the social pressure. I cannot think of many other activities that are nearly as significant for our personal welfare and for that of our Jewish people and the American culture as well. If all Jewish children received a substantial Jewish education and if, benefiting by that example, all Jewish adults made Jewish study a continuing part of their lives, our people would be sure to survive and to continue its creativity. (Would that our educational efforts had such intensity and continuity now!)

But, though Jewish charity and education have for decades aroused the loyalties of many Jews and fostered a meaningful continuity of the Jewish people, they are not self-justifying or even self-sustaining.

Our tradition of giving is commendable, but it does not thereby make clear why one ought to continue to give disproportionately to Jews or to all men under specifically Jewish auspices. A previous generation found generosity a means to obtain status among Jews. Today many of us aspire to recognition in a broader community. So we prefer to endow universities rather than rabbinical schools, cultural activities rather than refugee centers. Brandeis University managed its spectacular financial rise in American education precisely because it proclaimed Jewish giving to found a nonsectarian institution. On the ethical level, we can argue that mankind, not just the Jews, needs our help and our example. Education is certainly desirable, but why not give what little time and motivation we have to the far more immediate scientific, political and cultural questions that bedevil mankind rather than to Judaism? The issue is not charity or education, but the priority of their Jewish forms. We give Jewish charity and participate in Jewish education only as a by-product of a far more embracing sense of what it means to be a Jew. A Jewish sense of values brings them into being. For all their usefulness they cannot long exist on their own.

The immigrant Jewish *landsmannshaften* offer a pertinent analogy to the limits of pure ethnicity. The newcomers to the United States desperately needed one another in the early years of loneliness and penury. The friendly faces and reassuring accents one encountered at the meetings of his native community made the pain of being a greenhorn more bearable. But as the new language and culture became one's own, the old organization had less and less place in one's life. The various societies developed new activities to be of continuing use to their members: cemeteries, insurance, cultural programs. But, as time went on, this too was of no avail. The next generation had other needs and sought other social outlets. The Jewish *landsmannshaften* were only tangentially Jewish, so Jews today have little place for them. Jewish organizations and activities are, for all their power and necessity, not what ultimately keeps the Jewish community alive and well. Jewish action comes from an elemental feeling for the worthwhileness of Jewish living. Once we are committed to living as Jews, then wanting to be with other Jews, to give to and with other Jews, to educate for Jewishness, will follow. The question, then, is what will bring forth this more fundamental decision.

There was one great theoretical proposal in the United States —we shall discuss the State of Israel in the next chapter—to make our Jewishness purely ethnic. Chaim Zhitlovsky, the leading theoretician of the Yiddishist Movement, elaborated it in the period between the First and Second World Wars. He suggested that the Jews think of themselves as the first cosmopolitan, spiritual nation. Being unfettered by a land, they are free to link themselves with the aspirations of all mankind. With Jewish history supporting them and with many of its ideals captured in their very language, Yiddish, they could now live out the best of Jewishness among the peoples of the world. At the same time, they would keep alive their unique vision and the folk solidarity through which it endured, by a rich cultural creativity whose basic medium would be the Yiddish language. In Eastern Europe enforced social segregation helped such ideas to flourish. In the United States a voluntary sense of community might make the rise of a rich Yiddishist culture possible.

Zhitlovsky's thought influenced only a fraction of the immigrant community and is today largely of historical interest. But I think we may gain further insight into our own unconscious suppositions by looking back at the broad-scale social phenomenon which gave rise to it. In the 1880's and following, Jews, largely East European, began immigrating to America at the rate of a hundred thousand or more a year. They brought with them a unique outlook on Jewish existence. The majority were rather traditional in their Jewish belief and practice, though the more fully pious preferred European poverty to American secularization. The minority had already made the passage out of the ghetto and had channeled their messianism into one or another form of radicalism, usually centering around the labor movement and branching out into socialism or communism.

The decisive effect of these immigrant Jews in the history of American labor has long been recognized. But through their children they have also made a continuing contribution to liberal politics, a contribution that has not yet been as well understood. Yiddish-speaking socialists were not the only Jews fundamentally concerned with social justice, and one should not identify every lover of Yiddish culture with this variety of prophetic politics. Nonetheless, it affected far more than those directly affiliated with it. The continuing statistical disproportion of Jews involved in humanistic political concerns almost certainly derives more from Yiddish socialism and its satellite movements than from any other trend in American Jewish thought, such as the popularization of Hermann Cohen's philosophy of Judaism as essentially a universal, monotheistic ethics.

Where the socialists had substituted politics for religion, other

Jews put their faith in high culture, in Yiddish, to be sure. German Jews, who had already begun the pursuit of the arts in the nineteenth century never expected their community to produce a significant culture of its own. When the East European Jews began their efforts to celebrate Jewish folk artistry and create sophisticated works in Yiddish, the assimilationists at home and in Western Europe scorned their efforts as lowbrow and provincial. They condemned Yiddish as less a language than a jargon and deemed it incapable of serious cultural use.

The Yiddishists, however, refused to be snobs. They disclosed the creative ingenuity of the Yiddish folk song and the naïve charm of the Yiddish folk tale. They collected and analyzed and transmitted the most diverse ethnic materials—proverbs, jokes, and even curses—that still amuse and instruct one. They used these folk materials as the basis for a new literature. Isaac Loeb Peretz peopled his short stories with characters straight from the *shtetl*, or big-city Jewish quarter. Mendele Mocher Seforim preferred satire to compassion, and he used the whole of East European Jewish society as the background for his novels. As the century turned, East European immigrants brought to the United States a cultural movement less comprehensive in outlook than Zhitlovsky's version of Yiddishism was to be, but far more practical. They soon created excellent Yiddish newspapers, serious theater and light musicals, modernist literary circles and Yiddishist schools. Symbolically, Sholem Aleichem, the genius of this movement, spent the last years of his life in New York and not in Poland.

Since World War II the obvious decline in Yiddish culture—the Second Avenue theaters closed, the newspapers *Der Tog* and the *Morgenzhornal* shut down—has made it seem historical fact that American Jews can no longer build their Jewishness upon Yiddish culture. Yet a number of people have argued that Hansen's Law, the grandchildren reclaiming what the children discarded, may now apply to Yiddish. These observers have suggested that American Jews are sufficiently secure to reclaim their immigrant heritage and that, because they are such thoroughgoing secularists, Yiddish synthesis offers them a comprehensive and sophisticated model of what folk Jewishness could be.

American Jews do seem to be having a love affair with their grandmother tongue. *Fiddler on the Roof* had more performances on Broadway than *My Fair Lady. The Joys of Yiddish,* a book by Leo Rosten, sold over 100,000 hard-cover copies, and one publisher predicted more paperback sales for it than there are Jewish families in the United States. Yiddish is now taught at Columbia and other leading universities; it is an elective at the school for Reform rabbis in Cincinnati. Yiddishist schools, the Sholem Aleichem Folk Schules, have made the move to the suburbs and find backing from English-speaking parents who love Jewishness but are resolutely secular. Zhitlovsky's dream, one might conjecture, had only to wait a generation or so to come true.

Alas, this attraction to Yiddish looks more like a last fling of American Jewry than a marriage—or, to be true to our context, it is no *shiddach. Fiddler on the Roof* is so much more American romance than East European reality that the Yiddishists who are still around are generally appalled by it. Not only is the ugliness of the *shtetl* etherealized, its countervailing strengths are sentimentalized. And Leo Rosten's book does not teach Yiddish. It only tries to explain to an American reader what key Yiddish terms convey. A century of philologists and writers did not devote their careers to Yiddish in the hope that its jokes and vulgarisms would someday make *Yiddishkeit* sell. They worked to stimulate a genuine folk culture, not the sort of pop creativity that exploits nostalgia. The secular Jewish school in the suburbs is a far more positive activity, yet it is much more likely today to be teaching Hebrew than Yiddish. And it must suffer the indignity of preparing a child for a nonreligious *bar mitzvah.*

Leaving aside the practicalities of reviving Yiddish sufficiently to make it the medium of our Jewish existence, our root problem is not whether Jews are an ethnos but whether our ethnicity is all there is to Jewishness—or, to put it differently, whether the Jews are only another ethnic group with a somewhat abnormal experience. Though America has fortunately turned out not to be entirely a melting pot, its openness and mobility have little lasting place for rich ethnic existence as such. The European model—the Basques in Spain or the Walloons in Belgium—is hardly applicable here. Being Irish can be a great thing in New York City when one walks in its Saint Patrick's Day parade. (The Association of Jewish Hibernians is always a highlight of the march.) Yet what does the Irish-American way of life mean the rest of the year? Or in any other city? Or what will it mean some generations from now? If the Jews insist on modeling themselves after American Poles or Italians, they may survive for a while, but not in a way we would recognize as significantly Jewish.

South America provides an instructive example. It is experiencing an efflorescence of Yiddish culture, and critics say that some of the finest Yiddish poetry and essays ever written are being produced there. But, as in the *shtetl* culture, this outcropping of folk creativity is a direct result of isolation from the general culture, an isolation that is likely to be short-lived. Yiddish remains, almost exclusively, the interest of post-World War II immigrants, who continue to husband the spirit of Eastern Europe in the alien and largely closed Latin-American scene. Meanwhile, their children either wait to emigrate to the State of Israel or have given up interest in Jewish things. Yiddish culture, for all its virtues, is what Jews once lived, not what they might hope to live by today. It should be taken up and transformed by the culture that American Jewry creates. With the immigrant age past, we can see that it cannot simply be uprooted and transplanted from Eastern Europe here.

A more practical possibility derives from accepting the death of Yiddish yet continuing the Yiddishist's plan of centering Jewish existence around Jewish culture, pragmatically and eclectically defined. Many American Jews prefer to think of their

Jewishness as a simple enrichment of their lives. They enjoy the stories of Sholem Aleichem in English and respond to translations of Yehudah Halevi's medieval wine and nature poems or Martin Buber's retelling of Hasidic tales. They have books and records of synagogue chant, Hasidic melodies and Israeli songs. With all affluent Americans now interested in art, they have taken to buying old Menorahs and Torah pointers, as well as contemporary paintings and sculpture. Indeed, Israeli artists have had to turn from their own interests to supply the market for picturesque old Jews or young soldiers standing at the Western Wall.

And Jewish organizations now often prefer art shows to their old fund-raising favorites, bazaars and rummage sales. Jewish choruses and dance groups abound. Jewish books, fiction and nonfiction, lay and academic, on every conceivable topic, have never been published as widely as in recent years. Given these resources, there is no need to cultivate any broader and more old-fashioned style of Jewishness. We simply need to take advantage of our available cultural materials, and they are many. With a little effort we could multiply their number and increase their quality. Why not utilize them as a splendid means of enriching our lives and simultaneously preserve our Jewishness by our love of Jewish culture?

That is appealing—and an obvious rationalization. Let us be honest. We have too many cultural opportunities already. We buy books we do not read, records we do not listen to, tickets to series many of whose events we miss. We have a continuous sense of guilt about the FM programs we cannot get to hear, the courses we were going to take and finish this year, the galleries we had promised ourselves to visit. And there is that long list of classics that we know we simply must read or see or hear. All that is only in regard to Western culture. We are even more ignorant concerning the rest of world civilization. How can we understand Asian, African, South American politics, if we do not know something of the spiritual ethos of those continents?

We are drowning in culture. Ever since it was freed from the wealthy there has been an increasing flood of it. Our problem is not enrichment, but discrimination. We are not deprived, but overwhelmed. With the world's riches before us, our question becomes, What is worth my attention? To what shall I give my limited time?

In the midst of that intense competition, the Jewish products, considered strictly on their artistic merit, cannot command high priority. Purely as art, purely as music, purely as literature, Szyk and Castel, Sulzer and Bloch, Agnon and Glatstein are worthy of our occasional attention, perhaps even of our continuing interest, but surely not to the extent of building a way of life around them. Enrichment presumes that the foundation has been laid elsewhere, and now something is added that increases the significance of the original. Hence, Jewishness as enrichment is again secondary and not the sort of foundation to our lives that, in the face of our loss of confidence in general culture, we turned to our Jewishness to seek. Considering what the rest of the world culture has to offer us, Jewish culture can hardly claim to be the focus of our attention and our concern. And some would argue that, by the standards of the world's creative artists, the Jewish cultural expression is, on the whole, second-rate and therefore worthy of only occasional attention.

This judgment contrasts oddly with much of our experience. We love many Jewish sayings and songs. We get a great deal out of the old classic Jewish books and modern Jewish experiments in dance and drama. The ritual silver and the mosaics talk to us, and we hope our feelings about them will be renewed in the coming generations. If that isn't simply a response to the artistry, then the only way to explain our attachment is to involve family loyalty, saying, "But it is our culture. The Jews are our people and these creations came from Jewish hands." Such sentiments only bring us back to our original problem. We were asking about the possibilities of a purely ethnic Jewishness. Jewish culture hardly justifies it. Like Jewish association or charity or education, it commends itself significantly only to those who are already seriously interested in Jewishness. Our culture is less the root of our Jewishness than one of its choice fruits.

If there is any hope for a secular interpretation of our Jewishness, it can hardly be based on our East European past or our American Jewish cultural present. It will derive from the State of Israel. First of all, the State of Israel is a living reality. More, it genuinely moves most American Jews. Though they would insist that they owe it no political allegiance and do not want to emigrate there, they feel closely identified with it. Despite law and logic, they know that when Mr. Eban addresses the United Nations he somehow speaks for them. That brings us to those deeply devoted Jews who see their Jewishness centering about the State of Israel. Such a Jew too, for all his Jewish loyalty and passion, I must insist, is still wearing a Marrano mask.

# CHAPTER 8

# The State of Israel as Our Center

If Eastern Europe is a fading Jewish memory, the State of Israel is a glowing reality. Our people has its homeland back, and Israeli influence now touches the life of every Jew around the world. Though Yiddish culture cannot serve as the core of an ethnic American Jewishness, perhaps Israeli arts and letters could do so. This would seem the most realistic basis for creating a secular Jewish life in the United States and it has much to commend it: an avowal of Jewish ethnicity; a love of the State of Israel and an appreciation of its culture; a desire to build a positive Jewish life in the Diaspora. I hesitate, therefore, to label it with that old Spanish term of derision, *Marrano*. Yet for all the sympathy I bear this position, for all the creative Jewishness I see among its exponents, I must point out its ultimate inauthenticity. Regardless of the appearance of a complete Jewishness in this secular style, I believe that the Jewish values that we have been clarifying in these chapters 'cannot adequately be embodied in an Israeli-based American Jewishness.

I begin with the premise that the State of Israel is the most explicit focus of Jewish unity and emotion in the world today. If anything, this estimate is an understatement. Nothing else in Jewish life comes close to it. I do not think this eminence is solely the result of the continuing military peril under which the State* has lived since its founding. The precariousness of its existence has, of course, made its triumphs more precious and deepened the affection and pride that Jews have felt for what has been accomplished in that difficult and embattled land. That Israel exists, that Jews have built it, that they have done so with ingenuity and endurance, stability and courage, that despite the most harrowing conditions they have insisted their state bear a Jewish ethos, that for twenty-five years now they have made steady progress in rebuilding Jewish morale and reclaiming Jewish life—all this and more has made Jews love the State of Israel.

The response of Jewish youth to the State of Israel offers telling proof of this attachment. Many a Jew who was deeply shaken by the outrages and traumas of the 1940's has worried that the younger generation, which does not remember the birth struggle of the State, would not feel deeply concerned with it. Indeed, the young did seem to take it for granted. They were not visibly impressed that after nearly two thousand years, the Jews had re-established themselves as a politically autonomous state. Since they did not remember what world Jewry had to go through to win statehood, since they did not participate in the

---

* My usage, "the State," is peculiar. Permit me to explain. The word "Israel" is the most suitable term for the Jewish people as a whole, as, for example, in the most famous Jewish declaration, *"Sh'ma Yisrael . . ."* —"Hear, O Israel, Adonai our God, Adonai is One." To use it also as the name of a particular political entity can only cause serious confusion. Zionist theoreticians want that identification of the people with the state. I think it wrong in principle. Hence, in my writing,.when I say "Israel," I normally mean our people, the Jews, wherever they are. When I mean the Israeli political entity, I say "the State of Israel" or, when that becomes cumbersome, "the State."

triumph of its attainment, how could the State mean as much to them as it did to their elders?

These apprehensive questions received a decisive answer in the response of world Jewry to the Six-Day War of June, 1967. The lesson of those anxious days of May and climactic days of June is unforgettable. Almost to a man, American Jewry was aroused, active, eager to do something for their Israeli brothers. One might have expected an emotional reaction from older, involved Jews. What was overwhelming, to them probably as much as to anyone else, was the number of peripheral, even hidden Jews, particularly young people on college campuses, who stood up publicly and, using the telltale first-person pronoun, asked, "What can we American Jews do?"

Like all great moments, it passed. The old apathies and resistances returned. Yet, what happened was real and remains significant. The older generation need not worry so much about Jewish youth's lack of appreciation for the meaning of the State of Israel. What seems like indifference in them is only an indication of how natural it is to them, of how organic is their relationship to it. Their whole lives have been accompanied by accounts of its growth and productivity, its heroism and its indomitability. They do not share the anxiety of their elders, because they grew up with the State of Israel and have healthier attitudes to it and all things Jewish. Each summer now they join ever-increasing numbers of tours to the State, and the interest in spending a college year there has led, in addition to the foreign-student programs at the standard universities, to the establishment of an American College in Jerusalem. At home, while they ignore Zionist organizations as they do most other institutionalized activity, they have instinctively resisted the leftist effort to turn their anti-Vietnam War sentiment into anti-State-of-Israel sentiment. Some observers believe that a not insignificant reason for the collapse of the New Left movement in the early 1970's was its inability to attract strong Jewish loyalty to its radicalism when that involved condemning the Israelis as imperialists and aggressors.

Today the State provides what seems to be an absolute, unambiguous answer to all the problems of Marranohood. Become an Israeli. Come to the Land of Israel, speak its language, tramp its soil, help its development, live among your people, and you will know what it means to be fully a Jew. There alone can you know it in the fullness of your life rather than in hours snatched for Jewishness from the steady rush of Gentile existence. In the State of Israel, reading a newspaper, arguing about politics, going to a concert, watching a parade, even making one's business profitable, are all "Jewish" activities. Here every constructive act strengthens the Jewish people, and it is one's own people, not another group, that sets the standards by which one lives. By comparison, the most densely packed ghetto with the most inner-directed Jewish community elsewhere seems inauthentic.

So the Hasidim today arouse great sympathy for their complete devotion to their Jewishness. Yet they gain psychic space for their inner Jewish life largely by consciously withdrawing from the greater society. Their intense Jewish existence, mainly built on strict observance, is, in fact, substantially created by working at being different from the *goyim.* The Gentile society has its effect on them, though it is a negative one. They are not simply living as Jews on their own terms. A similar situation is seen in mainstream American Jewry. We are most effective educationally in the camp setting. Only by withdrawal from American life and the establishment of special but transient Jewish communities can we bring the Jewish ethos alive. Israelis do not have to step out of their society to discover their Jewishness.

The call for *aliyah,* for immigration to the State of Israel, makes many American Jews recoil. Normal love of country does not demand such a visceral reaction. But the issue is scarcely rational. Rather the old Jewish insecurities here powerfully reassert themselves. We become anxious lest Jewish emigration arouse suspicions concerning the loyalty of those who remain. If a sizable number of American Jews prefer to live in a Jewish state, and if those who do not themselves go encourage others to do so, will that not indicate that Jews do not consider themselves fully at home in America? Should our Jewishness alienate us that much and press its claims on us that hard? Such anxieties have been so widespread among us that American Zionist leaders have spoken most loudly for *aliyah* when they were out of the country attending international Zionist meetings.

I think there is just enough truth in these fears to keep them from being considered symptoms of paranoia. Still, if American democracy is reasonably secure, it should allow for some Jews deciding that they can best live as Jews in the State of Israel. If it is not that stable with respect to its latent anti-Semitism, then all the more reason why Jews should consider emigration. In any case the number of American immigrants to the State of Israel reached a new high in 1971, cresting at about ten thousand, the very figure David Ben-Gurion had called for some years before and for which he had been called a dreamer. Two reasons have prompted this movement.

The first stems from disillusionment, the cooling of the Jewish passion for America. Americans generally, and so Jews among them, have now had driven home to them the many failures of our civilization. America uses people mercilessly to give them its admittedly unparalleled standard of living. It cannot find a way to integrate many of its citizens into its productivity-oriented regimen, so it treats them like waste and can only think of them as if they were a facet of the pollution problem. Reforms are difficult, for our troubles arise from the system itself, not merely from certain effects. The symptoms abound. George Wallace built his national stature by moving on from racial issues to some of the legitimate questions raised by frustration of the old hopes of social progress. And if George McGovern did nothing else, he rescued most of the followers of Eugene McCarthy, who had become heavy with despair at the possibility of revamping so vast a structure. Some prefer to emigrate to the countryside to establish communes or live in person-oriented communities. So, too, it has become possible to think of living in countries less permeated by technology and thus less depersonalized—Canada, Australia and New Zealand.

In contrast to the *anomie* of America, one feels a sense of usefulness everywhere in the State of Israel. Even casual visitors are impressed by the pervasive sense of purpose among its inhabitants. One gets the sense that not just the politicians and the social workers, but the whole citizenry is shaping the society—and knows it. Simply by being there, by going about one's daily round, by living out the ordinary patterns of life, one is personally making the Jewish state possible. In the face of the Arab military threat and the occasional terrorist's bomb, living on the beleaguered soil is a daily act of heroism. In the face of the Arab numbers, adding another Israeli family raises Jewish morale and promotes Jewish survival.

Besides, Israeli society is cooperatively organized. Though a small nation and dependent on industrialization, the Israelis seem determined to make human welfare, not gross national product, their primary concern. From the beginning they utilized a Scandinavian style of social welfare, so that the benefits of the new society might be shared among all its members. The Histadrut, the giant labor cooperative with its far-reaching industrial activities, is the largest business factor in the life of the country. And whether years ago for Iraqis or today for Russians, tax policy is determined not only by defense and development needs, but by the need to rescue Jews. No wonder American Jews have been attracted there.

This new, wholehearted Jewishness, it should be pointed out, is available not only for those who become Israelis but for those who are planning on it. While they remain in the Diaspora, they can lead a Jewish existence informed by their commitment to migrate to the State. Their life is now focused on their Jewishness through their preparation. Acquiring a useful vocation, learning Hebrew, studying about Israeli towns or communes where one might live, becoming familiar with the economy in which one will work, and gaining familiarity with the politics in which one will be involved, may take place in Gentile surroundings. Yet it is an authentic form of Jewish existence. No wonder David Ben-Gurion insisted that only those planning to live in the State of Israel should call themselves Zionists. And their Zionism would indeed be a Jewish way of life.

We shall return to these ideas later. At the moment I only want to point out that, appealing as this form of Jewish existence may be, it has little relevance to a Jew who plans to remain in the United States. And that is what American Jews in their millions propose to do. Hence they do not see their Jewishness as essentially a preparation for *aliyah*. However, there are many Jews who feel that it should be possible to build a worthy pattern of Jewish life in the United States on the basis of Israeli culture. And in what follows, I take for granted all the positive things I previously said about Jewish ethnicity. Here I only want to consider how Israeli culture might become the dynamic center of our American-Jewish ethnic life, thus providing a living core around which all our other ethnic activities might grow and flourish.

One possible misconception of this stance must be quickly dismissed. I am not speaking of participation in a Zionist organization. The impact of such groups on their members' lives is as questionable as their emotional tie to the State of Israel is not. Hadassah, Pioneer and Mizrachi women at least try to study as well as raise funds. The men's groups are as vital as one would expect of firemen called into action about once every ten years. It adds to the difficulties that the national and international officials are all old worthies, still demanding the rewards of pre-State faithfulness. The only thing more unrealistic than the notion that Zionist-organization life is meaningful is the paranoia that sees organized Zionism taking over the American Jewish community. Almost all American Jews love and feel some identity with and responsibility toward the State of Israel, but the Zionist movement today seems largely a self-serving anachronism. No wonder the new executive board of the Jewish Agency for Israel found it desirable to supply one seat each to the American Conservative and Reform movements.

The most appealing ideology of a secular Jewishness based on the Land of Israel and serving world Jewry was presented in the writings of Ahad Ha-am, the great Hebrew essayist of the pre-World War I period. He proposed the influential vision of a rebuilt homeland serving as a spiritual center for all Jews. Its character was not religious, for Ahad Ha-am was a complete unbeliever, as was typical of Zionists in that period. Deeply devoted to the Jewish people and its tradition, he envisioned the Jewish state primarily as an exemplar of Jewish culture. To keep its standards suitably high, he disparaged mass migration and small colonization, and advocated the training of an elite who might properly lead in establishing a society centered about high culture. With such leadership the Jews could properly establish their folk existence and authentically express and cultivate their folk distinctiveness.

Ahad Ha-am believed in folk psychology, that each people had a unique bent or talent. The special genius of the Jews, he felt, lay in the realm of ethics. Hence, because its culture would be centered about ethics, the new state would have a culture that was relevant everywhere. Though many Jews remained in the Diaspora, they would be able to build a productive Jewishness by attaching their spiritual life—for Ahad Ha-am, the life of culture—to the creativity of their revitalized homeland. Receiving positive Jewish values and a sense of authentic self-respect from the spiritual center, they might hope to remain true Jews despite living among Gentiles.

Ahad Ha-am has had numerous disciples. They have dreamed of and labored for a Diaspora culture nourished by a Jewish state. In their cultural Zionism they made Jewish music and dance, Jewish art and literature, the living stuff of Jewish identity. Long before there was a State of Israel their activities greatly expanded the means of American-Jewish self-expression. So much for history.

What we see before our eyes, now that the State is a quarter of a century old, is a superlative embodiment of much of Ahad Ha-am's aristocratic vision. The Hebrew language lives and permeates every level of Israeli society. In Ireland, Gaelic is a language for literati and fanatics. In the State of Israel the couple screaming at each other in the next apartment regularly use the seven classic constructions of the Hebrew verb. Neon signs and comic books, even the inevitable girlie magazines, all proceed from right to left. Hebrew has again become the daily language of every Jew.

Ahad Ha-am would have loved the fact that the Israelis publish as many books per capita as any country in the world. More important, these are not books written in French or German or Polish or the other languages of the authors' origins. (Israelis have so many linguistic origins that preparing translations between any two European languages is one of their important export trades.) Almost all Israeli books are in Hebrew, a good many of them translations into the new mother tongue. The publishing phenomenon of the country is the *Hebrew Encyclopedia*. It drew so many buyers that it could finance more volumes than planned. This has drawn more customers and more volumes, so the end of the *Encyclopedia* is still probably not in sight.

Israeli literature is less a leisure pastime than a national resource. When Shai Agnon won the Nobel Prize for Literature, Israelis considered it as much a recognition of the cultural maturation of the State as an acknowledgment of the unique genius of Agnon's work. He did not write in modern Hebrew, but adapted the rabbinic Hebrew idiom to his tales of the recent and distant past. More typical Israeli authors have had a critical role in expressing and directing the national spirit. One can readily trace the fluctuations of Israeli concern through its established figures. Haim Hazaz, for all his attention to the Yemenite community, has articulated the need of the pre-State settlers to break from the old, transcendental emphases of Jewish history and establish a new national spirit; S. Yizhar's novel *The Days of Ziklag* caused a sensation after the Sinai Campaign of 1957 with its rejection of simple nationalism and its emphasis upon the individual will and conscience; Aharon Megged and Moshe Shamir continued the turn inward and away from national issues.

Today, with the Six-Day War behind them, young writers once again begin to ask social questions. Avraham Yehoshua, considered by some the most important young writer, again and again wonders in his war-weary stories, about fathers killing sons and the continual frustration of creativity. For twenty years now, the annual meetings of the Hebrew Writers Union have featured argument and recrimination over the sad state of Hebrew literature. In a perverse way, they testify to the strides that Israeli culture has made. Though there are many complaints, the criteria of demand would have pleased even so elitist a critic as Ahad Ha-am. One is left with the impression that, since the Israelis no longer expect divine relevation, the poet and the novelist should surely be taking the place of the prophet.

Through everything runs the love of the Bible. What opera is to an Italian or theater to a Frenchman, the Bible is to the Israeli. Literary classic, historical record, linguistic standard, geographic companion, humanistic resource—it is all that and much more. Not to be able to quote it is as much national insult as personal ignorance. Not to recognize its overtones in Israeli diction is to miss much of the beauty of what is being said. When the International Bible Contest is held, the entire country seems to follow the proceedings, and then everyone challenges someone else with the number and exact location of the exceptional names for God used in the book of Job or the like. Archaeology is a related madness, and Israelis take it for granted that their first chief of staff, Yigal Yadin, had in fact been trained as an archaeologist, and that their present Defense Minister, Moshe Dayan, suffered his most serious injury in recent years when a wall collapsed in a dig he was visiting, perhaps to add to his famed collection of ancient artifacts.

In Jewish scholarship Israeli students now hold the lead. Two generations ago one had to know German to pursue advanced Jewish studies. Today the essential non-English language is Israeli Hebrew. Soon no Protestant or Catholic professor of "Old Testament" will consider himself fully qualified to teach without some personal acquaintance with the Holy Land, familiarity with its major archaeological sites and a sense of how the Holy Tongue functions in its traditional setting. The Hebrew University Library is the finest of its kind in the world, and its growing archives on world Jewry will soon be indispensable to students of Jewish history. For some years after World War II it was difficult to find a set of the Talmud. Today one can choose between several Israeli editions and then, for accuracy, utilize the new listing of manuscript variations—projected to forty volumes—and follow up one's topic in Jewish law through the presently available fourteen of the twenty anticipated volumes of the *Talmudic Encyclopedia*. In brief, the center of world Jewish publishing is the State of Israel.

Once on the land, one gets the impression that Jewishness permeates the very air. In any other country, hiking is a pleasant way of passing time. Here to visit places like Megiddo and Gaza is a commentary on the Bible, to stop at Tiberias and Safed a reclaiming of one's roots. Time too is Jewish, for here one lives by the Jewish calendar. The Friday afternoon slowdown signals the coming of Shabat. Suddenly there is almost no traffic—no movement of cars, no noise and stench of trucks and buses—only people walking home, with little bouquets of flowers in their hands. All during the Saturday daylight hours an American Jew cannot forget that this is the day designated for refreshment and rest. I grew up in Ohio, where every December deluged us in Christmas so that, for survival's sake, we turned the eight days of Chanukah into high holy days. I can therefore well imagine the quiet Israeli pleasure of letting Chanukah remain a minor festival. And what a joy it must be when everyone knows Pesach or Shavuot is coming, and they come in the proper weather.

But the most extraordinary creation of the State of Israel is its masses of free Jews. The native Israeli does not grow up as a minority alien. He does not gain his basic image of himself as Jew through questioning, indifferent or hostile eyes. He need seek no special privileges to be himself. He grows up among his own. He speaks Hebrew naturally, loves the Bible naturally, follows the Jewish calendar naturally. Proud of Israeli accomplishments, he moves in the world with the easy step of a man who is sure of himself. Sometimes we American Jews are amazed by his casual self-confidence. Sometimes he seems typically aggressive to us, but we wonder whether we are reacting from our own insecurity which takes the form of diffidence and blandness, or whether his arrogance is a mechanism of his proud struggle to survive.

The Israelis and their culture are personally available to Jews all over the world in a way not even Ahad Ha-am could have imagined. We can go from any major American city to Tel Aviv faster than he could make his way from his Ukrainian home to any of the great European universities he tried to study at, always in vain. Soon, by virtue of supersonic planes, Lydda airport will be six hours from New York. With perhaps a hundred thousand American-Jewish tourists visiting each year, the State and its culture are already a living experience to a very large number of American Jews.

These trips have enabled many of us to experience how the State of Israel is the center of world Jewry. To begin with, to tour Israel is to be infused with an instant and durable pride. One has only to see those miserable, arid, rocky Judean hills cut by the sudden straight green line where Jews have planted trees or crops, and many things fall into place. All Isaiah's images of making the wilderness fertile, all the memories of coins clinking in blue-and-white boxes, join in a surge of admiration and hope. And if the hills are an experience, what can one say about the people? So many Jews, from so many places, so free.

If you want to know modern Jewish history firsthand and have the strength to hear of our travail, ask any non-Sabra, "Where did you come from?" Each one has his tale. Mostly they are humbling. We do not know whether we could have borne what they bore. We wonder whether we would have had the strength to live on and build as they have built. We marvel at their hope, their refusal to despair, their insistence on living for the future though not forgetting the past. And now there are the Russian immigrants. How did they survive their unprecedented cultural genocide? Where did they find the courage to try to emigrate? What miracle brought them out? We may come to the State of Israel proud of what we have donated to it. We leave as its grateful beneficiaries.

Yet, for all that the State of Israel and its culture can mean to us—and I hope I have made plain that I believe it can mean much to us—I do not see how it is realistically possible for our American Jewishness to derive from it. Our experience of this relationship during these past few decades is admittedly brief, but not unsymptomatic. We may love the State of Israel and be greatly enriched by it, but it becomes increasingly obvious that we cannot function as Jews by trying to live a vicarious Israeli existence on American soil.

Let us begin with the practical. Despite all our enthusiasm and support for the State of Israel, and despite even our visits, most American Jews have not learned Hebrew. The number who have even a reading knowledge is almost negligible among our five and half million increasingly well-educated community members. *Hadoar,* our one struggling Hebrew weekly, has about 5,000 subscribers. When the immigrant Hebrew writers die off, who knows whether there will be enough American Jews who are able or even enough interested to keep that major effort at Hebrew culture alive?

Fortunately for us monolingual Americans, English is an official language of the State of Israel. As tourists we can feel easily at home there. But we cannot have any culturally fruitful relationship with the Israelis unless we are at ease with their language. The *Jerusalem Post* gives one Israeli news. For the flavor one must read, say, *Maariv* or *Haaretz*. To hope that American-Jewishness can center about Israeli culture while most of us remain unable to read its books or magazines makes no sense. I deplore this situation, and I believe that we must do very much more than we have done to encourage the study of modern Hebrew. To begin with, we need a Hebraist elite as the nucleus of a movement to make the language live here. But the present status of Hebrew in America is disclosed by the fact that, "Yerushalayim Shel Zahav" ("Jerusalem of Gold"), the most popular of all recent Israeli songs, produces waves of sentiment in people who haven't the slightest notion of learning the words.

But even if we were all competent Hebraists, would this itself make us significantly Jewish? People like Eliezer ben Yehudah, the fanatic who more than any other man turned Hebrew into the daily language of the Jewish settlements in Palestine, thought so. They believed that there was a certain indoctrinating power unique to each language and implicit in it. Hence, as one became familiar with its sounds and vocabulary, its distinctive grammar and syntax, idioms and nuances, one progressively entered the spirit of the people. Language shaped the folk as much as the folk made the language. I see some virtue to that theory. Biblical Hebrew is highly verbal and is not given to abstraction. Deeds concern it more than the cultivation of some sort of inner life. Whether the language shaped the Jewish preference for action over transcendental meditation, or vice versa, or both emerged together, I doubt that we shall ever know.

In any case, I also doubt that using a language gives one any substantial identity. With the world so radically united, it is difficult to think of any given language as much more than an instrument of communication, such as the various languages are now in Europe. Two personal experiences illustrate this point. Abraham Harmon, formerly the Israeli consul in New York, first brought the point home to me when he began a speech to a conference of Jewish educators with some remarks in Hebrew, to this effect: Gentlemen, I know that many of you would like me to speak Hebrew as an example that the language lives. Now that the State of Israel has existed for a number of years there can be no question about that. Hebrew should be used for communication, not for demonstration. Since the former is my purpose here, I shall speak in English. And then he did.

Some time later a personal experience in the State of Israel confirmed this attitude. One of my major goals there, one summer, was to be able to read the daily newspaper with some fluency. Day after day I worked away at the technical terms which were unfamiliar to me. The political ones—*terrorist, hijacking, informed source*—came rather quickly. Those of economics and sports came very slowly. Then one day, in the middle of my reading, I suddenly realized that at home I would never spend my time reading such stuff! I really didn't care about new fringe benefits in the Haifa tire plant or the conflict over rules in the all-Israel soccer league. So the result of my increased Hebrew competency was that I could treat my Israeli newspaper the same way I treated my daily *New York Times*—I could skip most of it.

The same judgment would probably follow in the realm of high culture. Once we stopped marveling that it was expressed in Hebrew, we would discover little content that is not already available to us in English, thus far, in generally superior aesthetic form. But I cannot attach as much importance to high culture as did a generation that did not take doctoral degrees for granted. The ultimate question is not being able to create novels and plays and poems, even good ones by international standards, but having something to say in them. In this respect, Israeli culture tends to serve diverse ends for Israelis and for us. They have little or no question about their Jewishness. Their land, their language, their daily lives, seem to make it quite clear. Hence, they tend to take the question of their distinctiveness for granted, and they utilize the universal forms of Western culture to express their general human concerns. Meanwhile, we search for their specifically indigenous Jewish qualities and experiences.

In music, art and literature, the Israeli artists are quite international in style. To hear Ben Haim's music at Lincoln Center or to cross the street and admire Agam's stainless-steel sculpture on Juilliard's terrace, one would not know the artists were Jews —or, under normal circumstances, care. Good art speaks for itself. But if one is looking for help with one's Jewish identity, the experience is almost totally useless. Amos Oz's best-selling Israeli novel *My Michael* was recently translated into English and received fine reviews. Much of the novel, its concern with the inner life, with middle-class marriage and petty-bourgeois relationships, could have been written anywhere. And when it touches Jewishness it is in terms of special Israeli problems, the conflict between the Zionist fathers and sabra sons, or the relations between Jews and Arabs.

For the Israeli author cultural universalism is in no way a contradiction of his particular Jewishness, for that is essentially national and hence taken for granted, as a French novelist takes the distinctiveness of his milieu. Our American-Jewish situation is quite different. Standard American phenomena permeate our everyday life to such an extent that what is thrown into question is our specific Jewishness. Thus we come to Israeli culture seeking that which might distinguish us as Jews. And once we move beyond the language, we are disappointed. We seek the indigenous and find mainly the cosmopolitan.

I offer a somewhat humble example. Shortly after the founding of the State of Israel, many a Jew, anxious to identify with its culture, bought its craftwork to display in his home: a turquoise enamelware ashtray, or a pair of bookends, or a fruit bowl. At the time there was little Jewish art or folk handiwork. But we had been told that our Jewishness would be enriched by filling our homes with Jewish art objects. Loyal to this concept of Jewish culture, we placed such pieces around our homes. Now that Israeli products are more plentiful and visible, their existence is, as such, no longer a matter for Jewish pride. So our attitude toward the endless varieties of turquoise bottle openers and paperweights and coasters has changed. They no longer speak of Jewishness. They are only other imported things.

The Israelis, recognizing the difficulty, have responded. They now decorate them with Hebrew words, contrived tribal seals or the signs of the Zodiac complete with Hebrew name. They must tack on a Jewishness the article no longer carries. And, need I add, in the State such items sell only to tourists or exporters. The opposite effect has struck many a lover of the Hebrew language and its supposedly implicit spirit. The Israeli radio is far more likely to utilize it for rock-and-roll or store advertisements than for programs that express the lasting concerns of the Hebrew ethos.

I am arguing here that Ahad Ha-am's dream that Israelis would create a culture of such rich Jewishness that, received in the Diaspora, it would sustain authentic Jewish life there is most unlikely to occur. For the Israeli, his culture is a seamless extension of his Jewish life on the land, in the State and via the ancient Jewish tongue. For the Diaspora Jew, Israeli culture seems far less identifiably Jewish than are the circumstances in which it is created. The Diaspora Jew, lacking a Jewish environment, seeks Jewish culture to nurture his particular Jewishness, not merely to give him additional insight into the general human condition.

We can easily understand Ahad Ha-am's hopes. He not only believed in folk traits but he lived in a smaller world, where peoples, because of their relative isolation, could still be expected to produce distinct cultures. The Jewish State exists in another world. We see almost no evidence of ethnic psychology, and Israeli artists are not only in close contact with cultural developments in Europe and the United States, they want their creations to be judged by international standards. I do not doubt that some products of Israeli culture will be significant to American Jewry, but I do not anticipate much diminution of the difference between our needs and their output.

Perhaps we can see that best by looking at the realistic instance of trying to live by Israeli culture in the Diaspora—Israelis who have settled in the United States and Canada. The latter country recently indicated it had 22,000 Israeli migrants. The numbers in the United States are more difficult to ascertain. *The New York Times* has said that 10,000 or so Israelis now live in New York City. I have heard private estimates of 20,000 or more there, with perhaps 40,000 or so scattered elsewhere in the United States. If the Canadian proportions may be taken as a guide, these estimates for the United States are low.

In any case, after twenty-five years of statehood, substantial Israel Diasporas exist. In the Rego Park section of Queens Israelis are an easily recognizable ethnic community somewhat like Manhattan's Chinatown or Little Italy. One can get *pita* and *humus* and *tehinah* at the store to make *felaffel* and other Israeli dishes. *Maariv* seems to have been the major newspaper to survive the problems of transatlantic distribution, and Monday through Thursday WEVD broadcasts in Hebrew not only local programing, but tape recordings sent over by Kol Yisrael, the Israeli Radio service, including a weekly sports summary. The Jewishness of these immigrants is no problem, for it is solidly based on their recent Israeli origins. They congregate with their *landsleit,* share anxieties over the troubles of the homeland, assuage one another's guilt at having left it and mutually enjoy aspects of its culture.

But what of the Jewishness of their children and their children's children? How long will ties of Israeli culture keep the ensuing generations, now fully at home in the Diaspora, significantly Jewish? Their children will be born American citizens, grow up as primarily English-speaking Americans, and link their personal destinies, as their parents did, to life in the United States. Their old folks may still want to tune in to WEVD to listen to Hebrew broadcasts (as, a generation back, elders listened to its Yiddish programing) and they may care about reading *Maariv* (again, think of the Yiddish newspapers the *Forverts* and *Der Tog*), but why should the children bother? If to be an Israeli is a matter of nationality, they have accepted a new one, being an American.

If it is a matter of being a Jew, then I suggest that a few distinctive Israeli expressions or foods, or occasionally reading Israeli magazines or books, will not long keep a recognizable Jewishness alive. And as one sees Israelis who have struck roots in Pittsburgh or Atlanta or Denver, away from the dense emigre communities, struggle with the problem of their Jewishness, one quickly sees that Israelihood is not a viable form of Diaspora Jewish existence. American Jews are, therefore, only fooling themselves when they hope to found their existence on the basis of Israeli culture.

I propose to carry that line of argument one sensitive step further. I wish to contend that even for Israelis, a simple secular nationalism, for all the elements of authentic Jewishness it contains, is not free of the inauthenticity of modern Marranohood. We can apply to it the same sort of analysis we have used for American secularity. Again, the focus of our analysis is values and the separation of the outer, secular ideology of Israeli life from its inner commitment to humane existence. A somewhat dramatic example should clarify the continuing Israeli concern for a life of quality.

What if the State of Israel became a thoroughgoing fascist militarism? The idea is far-fetched, but by no means impracticable. Suppose the Soviet-United States disengagement in the area left Israel without substantial big-power support, while the Arab pressure, abetted by rising oil revenues in an energy-hungry world, only increased. To survive, the Israelis might be forced to drastic measures, like the military takeovers so common in Latin America and Africa. And the army officers who were blamed for displacing Bedouin at Rafah, near Gaza, or defoliating Arab lands at Akraba on the West Bank, are proof that not all Israelis are safe from the high-handedness associated with the military mind elsewhere. Something of this, as a political possibility, has been seen in the slowly climbing support of Israel's right-wing

Gahal party. Gahal is not fascist. Menahem Beigin does not speak of the necessity of strengthening the people by uniting it in military discipline to the will of its leader, as did Vladimir Jabotinsky, the intellectual predecessor of Gahal. But Beigin's continuing call for a strong line against the Arabs and the Soviets is closely connected to Jabotinsky's strong-man politics. In a new international threat to Israel's survival—or a crisis which is so perceived—the aging Ashkenazic political establishment might be thrown out, and a fascist government, protesting its democracy, might be established. We have seen equally unexpected political shifts.

For an ordinary state this would be a backward step. For a Jewish state, which its Declaration of Independence proclaims the state of Israel to be, this is a disaster. World Jewish opinion would be outraged, and those Israelis who were true to the sentiments that founded the State would feel betrayed. It is one thing to exalt the virtues of the Jewish ethnos. It is quite another to say that it may ignore the Jewish ethos. I disagree with Ahad Ha-am that the Jewish people has a genetic talent for ethics, but I do believe that most Jews connect Jewishness with a commitment to values which I have loosely called ethics. To them an a-ethical Jewish society—worse, an unethical Jewish state—is simply a contradiction in terms. For Jews to organize themselves as a Jewish state is not thereby to exempt themselves from the problem of finding and fulfilling a Jewish sense of values. If anything, it is to raise the question in more acute form. Because the State of Israel has such power and must confront such power, it must, so to speak, be more Jewish in values than a Diaspora Jewish community. In this respect, the judgment of the prophets is quite contemporary.

The secularity of the State of Israel, merely because it works from a Jewish ethnic base, is not saved from the indictment we made of the secularity of Western civilization; it cannot generate and empower the values most Jews continue to hold dear, the values which seem to have been at the core of the Jewish tra-

dition over the ages and which are so threatened today. If David
Ben-Gurion and Golda Meir and many others of their generation
still identify high humanity with stringent secularism, that is because their sense of the terms still carries the overtones of pre-
World War I European intellectual circles.

When the Second Aliyah rebelled against its parents and their
Diaspora Jewish attitudes, including religion, they could animate
their lives by an ethical socialist vision that seemed to derive
simply from the nature of man. Their grandchildren have grown
up learning the lessons of *realpolitik* as taught by Arab bombs
and guns, and they have no countervailing experience of traditional Judaism or the pretechnological mood of European culture with which to modify their amoral pragmatism. Surely
Moshe Dayan and Teddy Kollek are not responsible for the
novels of their children but, even allowing for youthful overstatement, it is difficult to believe that the younger generation will care
very much about messianic goals even in secularized forms. The
creation of the new, nonreligious, Zionist man—the Israeli—has
succeeded so well that, in some ways, the average sabra is far
more secularized than the American Jew.

At the same time, the Israeli culture, now so attractively purposeful, is not immune to all the same problems of technologiza-
tion and materialism that have disturbed American Jews. The
Israeli development leads directly to them. To survive, Israel
must industrialize; with few natural resources it must specialize
in high-technology manufacturing. A. D. Gordon's ideal of re-
storing the Jewish soul by working on the soil now seems a
Tolstoyan fantasy. The *kibbutz,* once the ideological showpiece
of Zionism, not only attracts an increasingly smaller proportion
of the population, but is steadily turning from farming to manufacturing.

The widely discussed Israeli economic growth since 1967—
second only to that of Japan in the past few years—has led
not only to the discontent of rising expectations but also to a
recognition of the gap between the Israeli rich and poor. The

sudden resignation and return to office in 1972 of Yitzhak ben Aharon, Secretary General of the Histadrut, was indicative of the widespread unhappiness of Israeli labor with its share of the gross national product and its restiveness over defense demands that have kept from it the television sets, the air conditioners and the Volkswagens it desires. Coming from a more recent impoverishment, Israeli Jews are as anxious as American Jews once were to acquire all the goods and services that diligence might make available. All this has bred a materialism whose intensity is held in check only by the overpowering commitment to national security. So the wage-control system has created a whole style of illicit payoffs, while to get a reasonably speedy response from the government or Histadrut one must master the Israelis' discreet version of *baksheesh* or have *protektsiya*, contacts.

I am not charging that Israeli secularity leads to greater venality than that which we see about us in the United States. I only want to say that the appealing Israeli sense of national purpose should not be romanticized as a permanent quality of a Jewish state. What moves us so deeply is more a response to external danger than the expression of an inner, unified national consciousness. Perhaps only the need suddenly to save hundreds of thousands of Russian Jews could produce a sense of national purpose once peace with the Arabs comes or there is a major lessening of tension in the Middle East. Even that is doubtful, for the Israelis, under the social pressure of the current Russian migration, have begun to talk of the possibility of limiting immigration, previously an unthinkable idea. The greater truth would seem to be that the Israelis cannot escape the plight of man in our Western civilization, for they are fully a part of it. Their problem, then, like ours, is how to find and maintain the values that will make it possible to redirect society's energies in more humane directions. And they, like us, to place these values on a firm foundation, will have to reach for a sense of existence that transcends secular limits.

Jewishness as nationalism, Zionism, and the dominant Israeli sense of being a Jew which derives from it, must be adjudged another Marrano style. It calls forth an exterior Jewishness, one founded on soil and language and culture, yet it hides from the fact that the values it affirms reach to a transcendent level that commands and validates them. Jews adopted the self-image of nationalism from the nineteenth-century Italians and Germans who taught Europe the importance of political autonomy for every ethnos.

But Jewish existence cannot adequately be described in nationalistic terms any more than it can be described in that other nineteenth-century notion that the Jews are essentially a church. I think this inadequacy comes out most clearly in the notion, so often trumpeted by David Ben-Gurion, Abba Hillel Silver, and other spokesmen for the movement, that Zionism is essentially the modern version of Jewish messianism. Precisely. The Jews are indeed an ethnos, and their restoration to their ancient soil and their sovereignty over it is one of the great moments in Jewish history. But no state is the Messiah, and no state, as a secular entity, is capable of bringing the Messiah. I do not see how the American Jew or the Israeli Jew can long hide from the ultimate, transcendent reality upon which Jewish existence rests: God. So now the time has come to talk about Him and our relation to Him.

# CHAPTER 9

# When Institution Replaces Community

My friend Harry Gersh says that nothing makes Jews feel more uncomfortable than having to use the word *God*. I don't know whether he thinks that's a carry-over from the old Jewish practice of using euphemisms for God's name, like *Adonai* ("The Lord") or *Hashem* ("The Name"), or part of the Jewish sense that it is blasphemy to jabber about Him. In any case, I think he has nicely caught a symptom of our Marrano attitude toward God. Since we not only don't talk about Him much but, when we do, seem somewhat embarrassed by it—particularly in contrast to Protestants at a Bible breakfast or a meeting of Businessmen for Christ—we take ourselves to be rather unbelieving or agnostic. Yet, if we were totally unbelieving, I'm certain we could speak of God as casually as we do about angels or the devil. Most Jews, I think, believe more than they acknowledge.

Harry's comment is also revealing of the sensitivity of this issue. We have now reached the most secret layer of our Marrano

existence, the one we are at the greatest pains to hide from ourselves. Hence, we are highly resistant to any suggestion that any
such belief is, in fact, present in us. I am highly respectful of
such attitudes, since I take them to be connected with the old
Jewish experience that false gods are worse than questioning,
and that acknowledging God means making Him the standard of
one's life. Jews have known and cared enough about God not to
take Him casually. Nonetheless, I think that the same analytic
procedure we have used up until now may help us see in ourselves something that we doubted was there. I do not propose
now to prove that God exists—you would not believe me even if
you couldn't refute me! Rather I shall try to deal with some of
the attitudes that prevent us from seeing what we do believe.

And I shall not try to present a definition of God—hardly a
Jewish way of speaking about Him in any case—or to outline a
modern conception of God. Rather, I shall proceed without
speaking much about God, though He is the announced theme
of this stage of our analysis. We must proceed as heretofore, indirectly, taking as our basis the arguments people use to hide
from what I take to be their true selves. It has been my regular
experience as a theologian that not until our Marrano defenses
are down, not until we have acquired some initial insight into
what, even dimly, we believe, can we profitably discuss such sophisticated issues as the knowledge or experience of God, or His
attributes or nature. Gersh's law, that Jews are most uncomfortable talking about God, may have increasing exceptions. Nonetheless, discussions about Him regularly shift to complaints about
the synagogue and the rabbinate. So we must begin there, reserv-
ing the questions of personal belief to the next chapter.

I am convinced that much of the problem we have with God
is not related to Him but to the institutions that purport to represent Him. The problem is not God's absence, as the spectacular
collapse of the Death-of-God movement should have made evident. Just five years ago William Hamilton was saying that the
characteristic religious experience of our time was cosmic empti-

ness, the sense that God had disappeared. Those who joined him on the no-God bandwagon then insisted that all new conceptions of religion must begin with the primary datum: God was gone. Today He seems remarkably available—more powerfully so to Jesus Freaks, Campus Crusaders for Christ and converts to Lubavitcher Hasidism; more tentatively so, I think, to people who sense the intimations of transcendence in their lives and would like to know what they imply.

This mood of search takes many to Yoga or Transcendental Meditation, while, as I sketched out earlier in the book, it has led an unexpected number of Jews to inquire into their Jewish heritage. What stands in the way of many of these Jewish searchers, I suggest, is less Jewish theology than the character of American Jewry's institutional religious life. Sensitive people are, to use the mechanistic jargon of our age, turned off so regularly by our synagogues and our rabbinic style that they never find out what the Jewish heritage teaches about God and how that might relate to what they have sensed in themselves. In a technologized, increasingly amoral world they seek a teaching that would keep our lives steady in the pursuit of value and a community that would strengthen their resolve and influence society. The synagogue, instead of sensitizing persons, emphasizes decorum; instead of creating community, it builds an institution; instead of changing society, it serves itself. Let us consider those charges in detail.

Since our society increasingly treats us as one of a mass, we long for a place where we can be treated as persons, where our selfhood will receive validation and moral staying power. The synagogue should do that for us. Through its celebration of transcendence and its recollection of ethical endurance, it should uniquely be the means by which, from time to time, we touch the ground of our being and are reminded of the value of existence. But what the modern synagogue cares about most is corporate dignity. Pray too loudly, cry or shiver at your sorrow, or laugh at your joy, and people will stare at you. If an emotion moves you deeply, you had better repress it. You may want to express it, but that would be thought peculiar. You had better not even linger over a phrase in the prayers or an insight they have suggested. The service rolls on relentlessly and you feel guilty for having gone your deviant, personal way.

Consider the signs of proper decorum. Things must be stately and conducted with a touch of pomp. Voices should be deep, rich and resonant. Words should come slowly, solemnly and with heavy emphasis. By such rules one man or two dominate a silent majority, who are expected to be still, obedient and uncomplaining. They must forgo all spontaneity. Our assemblies have great dignity. But what of us, whose individuality has once again been subordinated to an impersonal, corporate need? Our synagogues are repressive so as to be impressive, whereas what we need is a service expressive of our true selves.

A few years ago I tried a small experiment in this regard. Trying to explain the conflict between style and content to a conference, I spent some moments uttering some semiheretical theological garbage while, without saying anything about it, loosening my tie, opening my shirt collar, scratching my neck and then slouching at the podium. I could then point out to my hearers that while no one would be much bothered by my rather senseless ideas, almost everyone would be disturbed by my breaking form. And that had indeed been their reaction. The only religious law Jews regularly enforce today is proper behavior. We will tolerate, even boast about, our rabbi, the heretic. But let him cultivate dirty fingernails, be gross at the table or socially vulgar, and he is anathema. We do not really care how much Torah he knows and teaches as long as he dignifies us in public—particularly when there are guests present. The same standards apply to our *bar mitzvahs*. The children may not know very much, but we are determined that what they do shall be done smoothly. If then, we seek a sanctuary for the individual life, we are at cross purposes with the modern synagogue.

The same disappointment touches us when we come seeking

community or social impact. Most of our life is spent with people in functional relationships; they work for us or we for them, or both of us for someone else. We try to personalize such contacts, but if one leaves the job, one generally leaves the people. The relationships are not so personal that they survive a move, generally from a neighborhood as well as a job. Even in our social activities, people mostly tend to use each other. In contrast, the synagogue should be a place where individuality is precious and where creating bonds of concern between individuals is a primary goal.

Apparently that was once high on the synagogue agenda. Since anyone may start a synagogue, Jews who could not find community in one *schul,* simply began another. My father recalled that in his *shtetl,* Sokolow, there was a *Schneiders'* (Tailors') *Shtiebl,* a *Schusters'* (Shoemakers') *Shtiebl* and a *Chasidic Shtiebl,* not to mention the big *schul,* to which everyone went on the major holidays. More, the synagogues always had study *chevrahs* (that untranslatable Hebrew-Yiddish term, literally, a companionship) which one could join according to the level of one's learning, say Talmud, Mishnah or the reading of Psalms. Paddy Chayefsky's *Tenth Man,* for all its appeal to audience sentiment, retains the sense of individuality become community that was characteristic of the traditional synagogue.

The modern synagogue, by emphasizing dignity, promotes very much more formal and impersonal relationships. Instead of *chevrahs,* it has committees or study groups. Of course, the synagogue is always happy to have someone work on its Membership or School Committee, but they are organized to do a job and are not much concerned to get people to know and understand each other. One can meet people at a discussion group and, depending on how much the rabbi lectures, one can get to know something of their ideas. But, while this is another chance to make acquaintances, it is a rare group that moves on from a shared experience to caring for one another. Perhaps the only places in the modern synagogue where human relations are as important as the task at hand are the much maligned Men's and Women's Bowling Leagues. A devoted bowler would insist on more serious competition. In these groups it is banter and camaraderie that are the primary attraction—though this is so relatively superficial a community relationship that it barely touches on what the synagogue might be doing for us.

The current mode of rabbinic operation does not serve us much better. Of course, the competent rabbi will try to remember our names, to ask about our children and congratulate us on the award we just received. He will visit us in the hospital and, if we ask to see him, make time to listen to us sympathetically. We appreciate that very much, and some few people in every congregation have got close to their rabbi. The trouble is that the way the rabbi normally functions does not create individuality and community but thwarts it. His personalism is often only a professional skill. The realities of his role appear most clearly in our general conventions concerning him. He is supposed to talk and others are supposed to listen. We try not to argue or contradict him. Mostly we avoid telling him the hard truth. Instead, we ask polite questions, and he answers.

He is important and we somehow are not. In his presence we defer to him and, if he is gracious, he will be cordial to us. The exceptional man can use this elevated status to help those who cluster about him to be more themselves and relate with some intimacy one to another. The curse of the rabbinate is that most rabbis use the role more to satisfy their egos than to create community. And the rabbi's sense of his own importance, his handling of his position of primacy, convince many that their individuality will not be enhanced by being in his presence nor will their need for community be fulfilled under his leadership.

The synagogue likewise seems to care more about itself than about Jewishness or the transformation of society. Despite years of satire and moralizing against it, synagogue board-of-directors meetings remain overwhelmingly concerned with money and administrative matters. Synagogue leadership means not greater in-

volvement in Jewish religious concerns but temple politics. Neither study nor worship ever involves people in such numbers or
intensity as does a bazaar or journal or art show. In contrast,
there are not only few people involved in synagogue-sponsored
community action projects but, unlike the fund-raising, it is difficult to find new people to lead and stay with them. These ugly
blemishes in synagogue life repel the searcher attracted by its
beautiful traditions.

Sentiments such as these have powered the efforts to create
new forms for Jewish community. Havurat Shalom, near Boston,
pioneered the many student efforts at living communally for the
purpose of better realizing Jewish fellowship in prayer and study.
The Micah Community of Washington has rather centered its
group life around personal-participation projects related to
stopping the Vietnam war and other social-ethical issues. A number of small, do-it-yourself, Jewish family groups have surfaced
near Philadelphia and other large Jewish centers. Not too long
ago there was almost no such extrasynagogal experimentation.
Today there are so many that we almost take them for granted.
They indicate, I believe, a rather widespread feeling that our
present-day synagogue and rabbinate are not responsive to the
quest of many Jews. One might well conclude that this discontent is not limited to the sensitive few, but extends much further.

Apparently, large numbers of young Jews are no longer doing
what their parents did, ending their alienation from the synagogue when their children are old enough for religious school.
In many places and varying circumstances in recent years I have
received the impression that many Jews are longing for a way
in which they could have community without institution. They
want Jewish companionship, but they are tired of organization
life. They know you cannot long be a Jew by yourself, but at the
moment they see no Jewish gathering place that does not kill
community for the sake of dues, reports, resolutions and buildings.

With all that granted, I do not see that any of the experimental forms thus far created will serve American Jewry as a substitute for the synagogue. The Havurot in Boston and elsewhere have done for some college students only what the camp experience in intensive Jewish living had previously done for Jewish teen-agers. Joint living arrangements seem unlikely to attract many people beyond the campus years. And that is the most promising of the experiments in community. Perhaps a Baal Shem Tov will arise among us and create a pattern of adult Jewish life as vital for us in America as Hasidism once was in Eastern Europe. Short of that, I believe we may hope that the synagogue, despite its present failings, can adapt itself to meet our present needs. I think that that is true because people, in large part, get the institutions they ask for. The Episcopalian-toned synagogue was brought into being because the Jewish community once wanted it. Now that our needs have changed, that style has outlived its usefulness. But, as we once created that sort of synagogue, there is no reason why we cannot now create one sensitive to personal needs and warm human relationships.

Our decorous synagogue is a product of the Jewish Emancipation. The Reform movement began in 1810 with Israel Jacobson's revolutionary synagogue in Seesen. Almost all the changes he introduced were aesthetic, for, as he said, he wanted to show that the Oriental outsiders could be proper Western Europeans. Instead of *a cappella* music, with its temptations to harmonic vagary, he introduced the organ, polyphonic music and the mixed choir. Instead of individual prayer within a general group procedure, he had a set pace for everyone in the congregation. Instead of the rush to finish a long service, he eliminated some prayers so that all might proceed deliberately and with greater concentration. Instead of chatter in the congregation, there was absolute silence. Instead of all the prayers in Hebrew, he prepared a number in the vernacular, German. And as the climax of the service, there was a dignified, uplifting address. The eye-witness account of the opening of Jacobson's temple repeatedly emphasizes the dignity that marked the event from the opening procession to the closing prayers. From that day on, decorum has been the chief means by which the old Jewish religious practices were domesticated to the ways of Western society.

The same demand for social adaptation made itself felt in the Yiddish-speaking immigrant Jewish community in the United States in the 1920's and 1930's. The Conservative movement, which first comes to vigorous life in this period, is best seen—sociologically speaking—as an instrument created to accommodate East European Orthodoxy to American tastes without being quite so Protestant as the Reform Jews appeared to be. The modern Orthodox synagogue comes last in this development, and in general it may be said that the synagogue took on the conventions of religious decorum in direct proportion to the amount of contact Jews had with Gentiles. In the Columbus, Ohio, of my youth, the 1930's, Shabbos services—once on Sunday—were stiff at the Reform temple, controlled at the Conservative synagogue, and occasionally unruly at the large Orthodox *schul*. In recent years when I have visited there, I have found the decorum gap to have narrowed almost to the point of disappearance. The Reform Jews have relaxed somewhat, and the Orthodox only rarely need to be called to order.

Despite American-Jewish differences over Hebrew, organs, the seating of women and shortening the service, we refugees from the ghetto were determined to be part of America. Since the church set the style for what Americans considered religious, we knew we had to take over some of the church conventions—we demanded a neo-Elizabethan prayer-English; we learned to read responsively and sing in unison; and we wanted rabbis who used big words and quotations from modern literature. For the sake of belonging, American Reform Jews even did away with *yarmulkes*.

But above all we wanted the order and silence that Americans affect in solemn assembly. So we forbade the children to run up and down the aisles, tried to stop people from walking in and out during the service, made chatting during the service a major social blunder, and finally brought into being the ponderous, elephantine style which now so oppresses us. It took quite a while to change. The old-timers insisted on doing things their way, and the regulars liked it the way it had always been.

Only, now that we have services dignified enough to calm the anxieties that every immigrant's child felt at his strange origin, we are dealing with a Jewish population that is native-born and reasonably secure in the general society. They want a synagogue that will express their Jewish feelings, not justify their presence in America. They do not need the phony dignity that comes from being stuffy. They prefer things loose and easy-going. They do not choose mohair sofas and tall celluloid collars. They want to relax and be themselves, including their Jewishness. For such people there is a generation gap between their and the synagogue's social interests.

We have done the same thing with our rabbis, creating a new type of rabbi to meet the needs of our Emancipation. Instead of a judge and teacher of Jewish law, we wanted a figure to mediate between the old Jewish traditions and the American society. With his first class in 1875, Isaac Mayer Wise, founder of the Hebrew Union College, insisted that Reform rabbis must have a secular college degree. We take it for granted today that most Orthodox rabbis have had college training, though, to the best of my knowledge, that is true of only the rare exception in the State of Israel. We also make it a primary requirement of the rabbi's performance that he get along well with the Gentiles, that he be "well accepted" in the non-Jewish community. A rabbi can hardly justify his existence these days by pointing to his activity with the National Conference of Christians and Jews or the Anti-Defamation League. Still, if he blunders in community relations he is likely to have put his job on the line.

With this new rabbinic role came an unconscious deal with the laity. As they knew and cared less about Judaism, he would be Jewish for them. More, they would consider it a major part of his rabbinic role to try to win them back to Judaism. The American rabbi thus became the first Jewish missionary to the Jews. Because the rabbi represented most Jews in duties they could not perform for themselves, he received from them a new and high status. The rabbi became a major community figure whose advice was to be solicited and listened to with respect, though not often acted upon. He was always seated on the dais, always asked to say a few words, always invited to meet the important people and invoke at the significant gatherings. In short he not only became the highest-salaried American clergyman but received an extraordinary compensation in ego-dues.

The rabbi, in turn, enhanced his own position by taking upon himself the ethos that had formerly belonged to and obligated the community. In theory, he might not be happy about the qualitative difference in Jewishness that now opened between him and the laity. In practice, his special status was based upon it. Hence, to this day, to gain the special advantages of the rabbinate, the rabbi is tempted to center Jewish life about himself rather than to create the sort of equality basic to a sense of community. Having come to expect the ego satisfaction of always being in the center of things, he finds it difficult to learn leadership by creative withdrawal. Yet the present arrangement, as mutually satisfying as it is unacknowledged, cannot much longer be tolerated. It has no Jewish validity, and it demeans the rabbi and laymen alike. What modern men, striving desperately to be persons, want from their religion is an encouragement of their maturity, not reinforcement of their infantile needs for dependency. We are left with a rabbinate that our fathers created in their quest for social integration, only we require rabbis who will stop being Jewish for us and indicate how, together, we can all be Jews.

I think the synagogue and the rabbinate can change their dominant modes of conduct because, in fact, they have already begun to do so. The concern to be a person was not born in the 1970's. It has been a persistent, if unacknowledged, factor in American cultural change since World War II. The suburban synagogue, now so largely under attack, should perhaps be seen as the transition institution between the dignity-conscious Emanuel-type cathedrals of the pre-War period and the personalist-community-creating bodies I hope will soon come into being. For all its present emphasis on etiquette and form, the suburban synagogue has sought to lessen the gap between the rabbi and the laity. Its sanctuaries are small; its pulpits not highly elevated; it often limits its size so as to enhance face-to-face contact; its officers and board are not self-perpetuating; its children come actively into the community with nursery school; its teen-agers can experience Jewish life at camps or conclaves; its youth groups experiment; its women study; its members insist that, above all, they want their rabbi to be a *mentsch,* a real person.

Think what might happen if we could take these somewhat random and undirected energies and make them the conscious transforming power of the modern synagogue and rabbinate. If we do indeed get the institutions we ask for, then consider what might happen if some Jews who consciously accepted their Jewishness came together as a group. They would ask the synagogue and rabbinate not to represent them to others but to help them live out their Jewishness.

Such a synagogue could stop worrying how beautiful its services were or by what sensational means it would draw a crowd. These determined Jews would consider both notions irrelevant to their interest in prayer, study and getting together. Their synagogue could not serve them by substituting decorousness for piety, or by saying the smooth flow of the service was more important than encouraging individuals to express themselves in prayer. It could not claim that unless it had a fancy building or a big budget, Judaism might die. These committed Jews would give that the lie, for they would not be Jewish because of the synagogue. If anything, the synagogue would be Jewish because it served them. And we may hope that, spurning formality and propriety but coming to be Jews together, they would reach out to one another so as to make new patterns of Jewish camaraderie possible.

Were the rabbi to serve such a group—Jews whom he did not represent to the world and to Judaism but only taught—his role would change decisively. Sermons and lectures would no longer be his major activity, as they are now and will continue to be just as long as he must know more and care more than anyone else. As merely one of a number of inquiring, active Jews, he could fulfill his responsibility by leading a *chevrah*—figuratively now, a combination Jewish discussion group and social club and seminar. With a cluster of believing Jews in the synagogue, it would be foolish to claim that Judaism centered on the rabbi and his personality. Thus he would no longer have to lead and succeed in everything. He would no longer need to continually tailor and project his ego so as to personify the attractiveness of Judaism and the decorum of Jewishness. Both would carry on without his being a "personality." So there would be a chance for him to withdraw from being the center of attention and make room for the ego needs of others. Such a rabbi could go back to being more of the guide and example that his traditional forebear was. Better, in a society of strangers and masqueraders, he could concentrate on being a person of full ethnic and religious depth. One thing is certain: with a few devoted Jews around, he would be a lot less lonely.

I cannot detail what such a personalized-communalized Jewish religious institutional life might be like, for I think it would in due course create its own appropriate forms of Jewish living. I can give one example of what such creativity has already produced: the Sabbath kiss. In American congregations, wherever men and women sit together, when the benediction has been given and the worshipers have said "Amen, good Shabbos" or "Shabat Shalom," husband and wife quite naturally give each other a kiss, and perhaps kiss their friends as well. This may seem trivial, yet it is our unique folk creation. No one knows where it began or by what authority people feel compelled to do it. Yet almost everyone kisses after services, for it seems an appropriate way of expressing our sort of Jewishness. It unites the joy of the Sabbath with the love of persons. It links Sabbath peace with peace in our marriage and peace in our home.

I confess that, from time to time, the kiss has been the most moving part of the service to me. Sometimes I have brought with me to the synagogue a block that some word or deed created. Reaching across such a barrier is not easy. Yet, standing in the sanctuary, having said the prayers, I have realized I must learn to love better. So when the service has ended and I have been able to give a proper Sabbath kiss, it has lifted from my heart a stone that I had not known how to be rid of. To find such peace is the Sabbath at its best. The Sabbath kiss is unknown to the traditional synagogue with its separation of the sexes and its teaching that affection should be displayed only privately. Yet for the modern Jew, the Sabbath can often come to life in this kiss as in nothing else.

I have every confidence that we can create much else that is valuable, if only we can find a few Jews who will as a conscious decision make their Jewishness the ground of their existence. But I think I have taken this analysis far enough. I only wanted to point out that the faults of our religious institutions are more a function of our social needs than they are of the nature of our God. If we are put off by the contemporary synagogue and rabbinate, I suggest He is far less to blame than we are. We have made them what they are and it is in our power to change them.

If anything, our discontent with these institutions is itself a hint of our concern for Him. If we did not have such high standards, we might well be satisfied with our busy synagogues and hard-working rabbis. Ironically enough, we are repelled by the synagogue for reasons just the opposite of those of a previous generation. They were so intent on its showing proper form that they hardly cared what anyone believed. We, however, are put off by all the attention to churchy etiquette because we somehow know that it does not serve Him properly. We sense, however, darkly, that He is the ground of our values, the measure of our conduct, the source of our endurance, the basis of our hope. He is too precious to us, too significant for our existence, to be represented so poorly. I think we reject His emissaries because we affirm Him. So let us now, quite directly, talk about believing in Him.

# CHAPTER 10

# The Ultimate Unity

The individual Jew and his sense of value, the Jewish people and its ethos, all come together in the Jew's relationship with God. Not any god will do, not even any god men have called the One God. He must, unlike some of the high gods men have worshiped, not be neutral to man and his actions, and surely not be a god who is malevolently inclined toward his creation. No, this God, the God of the Bible's revelations/discoveries, is Himself intimately involved in what the Hebrews called righteousness, so that this quality must permeate the life of man and society. Not every kind of relationship with this God will do—not one emphasizing contemplation, or concentration on inner feeling, or even immersion in prayer and sacred rites. No, the old Jewish relationship with God, for all that it assumed and commended a rich inner life of faith, was primarily one of action in society, reflecting the nature of this God being served. As He dominated creation, so His commandments were not in one area of life or in some few hours of some days, but in the totality of existence, personal and communal. The Jews called that relationship with God the Covenant.

The Covenant gave each Jew his sense of personal values, for the God with whom he stood in relation demanded a life of justice and compassion. It gave Jewish existence a lasting sense of social scope, for the Covenant existed between God and the Jewish folk, and with each individual Jew as part of that folk. No Jew, after Abraham, could claim he created the Covenant, that his participation in this relationship with God was, in effect, the result of his own ingenuity. He was born into it and educated to it by family and community. His individual moral striving was given power by the knowledge of what his people had endured to keep the Covenant alive and fresh and by its continuing insistence on doing what it could to bring the Messiah.

Jewish integrity comes with basing one's existence on the Covenant. The trouble is, we don't believe in God—or, more painfully, we *can't* believe in God though we may want to. This is what we say, and I do not see how one can deny the good and honest reasons involved. But in recent years, despite my respect for the sincerity of the people who voice these views, I have come to the conclusion that, for many, what they say is not altogether true, if what I see them basing their lives on is correct. For the last time, then, I want to suggest that this too is a Marrano façade. Let us try to find our way behind it.

There are two good reasons for not believing in God. How can people be asked to believe in what they cannot understand? From earliest childhood we are urged to question everything and withhold assent until reasonable assurance is achieved. What else can protect us from the fanaticism and superstition that have regularly caused great evil under the guise of serving great goals?

I fully share this attitude toward the application of mind to the assertions of faith, though I am not thereby brought to the agnosticism or atheism so commonly associated with it. I am far more severely shaken by the second reason—the modern version of the old Biblical complaint against God—the problem of evil. The facts of this world, most recently and particularly those of the Holocaust, are inconsistent with the existence of a good and powerful God.

These problems are so plain to us, they fit so well into the skeptical tenor of our age, that we have no difficulty in finding adequate terms to give them sophisticated and subtle form. I know professors of religion who have built academic careers by adding to our skepticism. But our lives contain faith as well as doubt. Finding the proper words to describe that faith is not easy. The "I believe with perfect faith" of Maimonides' Creed is impossible for most of us to say. And to assert that one knows anything with certainty is at once to make modern men suspicious. Speaking for myself, I know only moments, sometimes periods, of conviction—or better, assurance. But the times of questioning and skepticism return. I have come to accept this uncertain rhythm as the modern man's way of believing, less like a college diploma, won for all time, than a great love, significant beyond compare, but ever again challenged and, thus far, renewed. I speak, then, out of the balance of my experience, emphasizing the positive part of it, which I do not find commonly discussed.

The Marrano guises that we assume always serve hidden motives. Our stance of unbelief is no exception to this rule. Men in general have an itch to be rid of God. His commands are a nuisance, inhibiting one's urge to do only what one wants to do. His judgment is a burden, particularly when we are already so loaded with guilt that we do not want any more responsibilities to fail at. His forgiveness is unwelcome, for knowing what we ask Him to put up with makes us ashamed. Most annoyingly, admit His reality and you cannot shake Him. He may be nice enough to have around when we are quite strong or very weak, but since we are neither most of the time, He is too much to bear. Like our parents, He does not let us be ourselves until, oedipally, we kill Him off. I take it, then, that the present-day vigor of the practice of amoral freedom on the one hand, and of the rigid, fundamentalist churches on the other, stem from a common existential root. The former displaces God by the self and its cravings. The latter completely surrenders the self to Him. Neither understands the Jewish dignity of standing as a partner in Covenant with Him.

The Jews have special incentives to reject God. The first comes from His connection with anti-Semitism. God, after all, is a Jewish contribution to Western civilization, by way of Christianity, to be sure. When the wild tribes of Europe accepted Him, they had to accept His commandments and subject their primitive urges to His will. Psychoanalytically, such repression creates hostility. Since it cannot be expressed against Christianity, it emerges as hatred of Jews, the people who first found and served the commanding, righteous God. This underground reasoning has its parallel among Jews: if men could be rid of God, we could be rid of anti-Semitism. So, Jewish atheism has often been justified in the name of brotherhood, though its emotional foundation has been self-hate.

The stronger Jewish motive to deny God is our semiconscious identification of Him with the ghetto style of Jewishness. Believing in Him conjures visions of bearded patriarchs in black kaftans performing medieval rites. For many Jews still, to call someone "religious" means that he is observant, most often of the Sabbath or the kosher laws. Such people think of Orthodox Jews as the most "religious," Conservative Jews as less "religious," and Reform Jews as hardly "religious" at all. It may seem surprising that, despite the generations that have tried to display a modern style of Jewish belief, the inner images remain so archaic; but since this is a subrational level we are talking about, we must accept the compelling power of fantasy and image. If this dark history is the context in which we think about serving God, then it is clear why we do not want to associate with Him. We may be troubled by our culture's crisis in values, but we have gained too much from the Emancipation to want to go back to the ghetto.

Our resistance to God runs so strongly also because it has a certain moral justification. We assert ourselves against God so that we may take full responsibility for our actions. When religion emphasizes His omnipotence, man can easily sink into abject passivity, neglecting the power God has given him. The nineteenth century may have overemphasized man's goodness and inevitable progress, but it properly taught us to despise moral sloth. The return to the Land of Israel became a reality only when Zionists, who had learned this lesson, threw off the Orthodox insistence on waiting for the Messiah and started, on their own, to go to the Holy Land. The Zionist movement is part of the widespread awakening of man to his own power, an awakening that begins with the rise of the Industrial Age. In the surge of optimism that accompanied this new sense of man's potential, God was denied any significant place in the order of things. Human responsibility seemed to mean that God could have no power; humanism implied atheism. However, there is surely a great difference between our having autonomy and denying God any power in the universe at all, between our having a real role in things and insisting that it is possible only if God has none.

The Jewish sense of man's relation to God has largely avoided making either man or God the exclusive actor in history by insisting that they were partners. In the Covenant man was sufficiently independent of Him, not only to sin or deny Him, but to argue with God, as Moses and Job did, that He had not been faithful to the agreement. We modern Jews will want to take far more initiative in the Covenant relationship than our forebears did, particularly in pre-Emancipation days when oppression had reduced them to a comparatively passive state. We will want to explore Jewish duties to non-Jewish society, create new rituals and prayers, devise more adequate ways to think about God and delineate what He would have us do. We will want to be quite conscious and deliberate in shaping our relationship with God.

But such a disposition to change is quite a distance from the

atheism or agnosticism that demands that we dispose of God altogether. Responsibility should not mean the end of relationship.
Rather, as we have repeatedly learned from love and friendship,
if the other will not overwhelm us but will give us room to
stand on our own ground, it is precisely from what passes between us that a true sense of responsibility arises. Judaism believes that God is so powerful that He can give man freedom.
But in the Covenant which these partners then undertake, responsibility not only arises but is central.

Similar distinctions should be made about the legitimacy of the
urge to understand God. We surely need to try to comprehend
as much as we can, and traditional religion may not have worked
hard enough at the cognitive task—another sign of what we take
to be its human passivity. But this drive can be carried to a
misguided extreme. Since the identity of God, like that of the
universe as a whole, is beyond human comprehension, what
would your reaction be to someone who said he understood God
fully? I think the only proper one would be a suspicion of
megalomania. To understand God even reasonably well, one's
mind would have to be as great as the divine wisdom. If we may,
for the moment, equate reality with God, some philosophers,
from Parmenides on, have assumed man has such ability. In a
way, Hegel brought the process to a climax. If the reality in all
change is the Absolute Spirit and if the philosopher brings Absolute Spirit in its clever, dialectic working-out of all history to
full self-consciousness, then the philosopher and God, so to
speak, are one. Such is the triumph of philosophic rationalism—
and the revelation of its ultimate *hubris*. In contrast, I do not
see that we understand very much of anything real and complex
in this world. Some modern philosophical theologians, of whom
Bernard Lonergan may be taken as the most courageous example, have argued that even to deny rationality is to use one's
mind and thus affirm some canons of logic and judgment. I
think that is more a debater's victory than a reflection of reality.
Of course I propose to use my mind, but I do not find that that

process is necessarily orderly or that its procedures or conclusions hold from day to day. Sometimes I am fairly clear and certain. Mostly, I am not. The thing I am most familiar with, myself, I continually discover I know very little about. My mind is indispensable to my efforts to understand me, but it is not finally adequate to the task. The same is true of God. I am not at all surprised or dismayed that we understand relatively little about Him, the most encompassing of all realities.

Significantly, classic Judaism, particularly as contrasted with the formative period in Christianity, had little concern with understanding God. In the Bible and the Talmud there is no metaphysical speculation comparable to that of Greek philosophy or Christian theology produced during the same periods. Definitions of God are unknown to Jewish tradition, and proofs of His existence had to be borrowed from the Moslems in the Middle Ages. If the Bible speaks about "knowing God" and the rabbis talk about the supreme value of learning, neither notion has much to do with ideas of God or speculation about His nature. They are concerned mostly with the acknowledgment of His rule, which is signified by living by His commandments rather than trying to figure Him out.

I think it highly useful that some modern Jewish thinkers, notably Martin Buber and Franz Rosenzweig, have urged us to concentrate on developing a relationship with God rather than on speculating about Him. For them, faith in God is not a matter of ideas or a cultivation of ecstatic states. They rather ask us to care about Him and to base our lives on the intimacy we share with Him. Living, rather than cognition or sensation, is made primary. Moreover, thinking about God in terms of our relationship with Him helps us to see the reasonableness in His case of what we have experienced elsewhere—namely, that you do not have to understand someone fully to have a real relationship with him. If anything, our most significant relationships regularly disclose that what we believed to be a thorough understanding of the other is narrow and superficial and that he has complexities and depths we can never exhaust. In life, understanding must coexist with mystery.

There is great benefit in trying to understand the other in a deep relationship. Yet the more we mean to each other the less adequate our language is to express what we have known. Our ideas distort the truth, and we are forced to the purposeful ambiguity of poetic language to express what we have experienced. Judaism early recognized that God was ineffable, so Jewish thought was permitted to acquire differing, at times contrary, ideas about God. It could afford this freedom, because Jews could largely be relied on not to confuse the necessarily limited statements about God with His greater reality.

Moreover, the chief concern was not conceptions of God, but conduct. Today a similar freedom of thought exists. Mordecai Kaplan has written sharp polemics against Hermann Cohen's and Kaufmann Kohler's rationalist theories of God, accusing them of ignoring the social realities in which ideas arise; and he has decried Franz Rosenzweig's and Martin Buber's existentialist Jewish thought as irrational and hence unsuited to our time. However, he has never denied that they were Jews or suggested that their books be anathematized. So, too, the pages of our leading Jewish theological journal, *Judaism,* have never reflected one conception of God, but rather the diversity of views available in the community.

This line of inquiry does not yet bring us to the heart of our problem. Most people do not want to understand everything about God, but only enough to make belief in Him reasonable. There lies our difficulty; "reasonable" turns out to be impossible to define. One man's evidence is another man's question. What will easily be granted in one gathering of philosophers is the nub of debate in another. Very often these days argument consists in finding out what the other fellow will allow into the conversation. Congenial intellectual company comes to mean people who share your assumptions.

Analytic philosophers, who emphasize clarity of meaning and

limit discussion to ideas that might have some empirical proof or disproof, have almost nothing to say to phenomenologists, who believe the mind can abstract from its own thinking processes enough to understand the system by which our sense of reality is structured. Existentialists generally find the latter more congenial than the former, but not always. Each group—and others—appeals to what is reasonable. With such a diversity of standards about us, it becomes impossible to agree as to what a reasonable understanding of God would be. I do not wish to be unreasonable in talking about the reality of God, but I must point out that there is no longer a common, easily available standard of what is reasonable by which to judge statements about Him.

To my mind, however, many of the demands for a greater use of reason in relation to God have gone too far. I think a good analogy may be found in our attitude to sexual relations.

A generation ago the ignorance and fear surrounding sex were so great that it seemed a major act of human liberation to make the facts available to people. That has progressed to the point where the physical, even mechanical, aspects of sexual relations are dispassionately studied and reported. This is a valuable achievement in certain respects. It helps people who need guidance in the physical aspects of intercourse and who have suffered from faulty instruction in love-making because they have had to be their own teachers. But this gain has been compromised largely by a new kind of error. Because we can most readily analyze and quantify sexual activity when it is equated with orgasm—the Kinsey approach—we are led to believe that this is what it mainly is. Intercourse becomes orgasmic interchange; full sex life is plentiful orgasms; a good sex partner is one talented at orgasm giving.

As Rollo May has recently written, this mechanistic understanding of sexuality can become a major barrier to a fulfilling sex life. We become so involved with efficacious physical manipulations that we never make love. We pay so much attention to proper stimulation of the nerve endings that we cannot pay much attention to each other as people. Sexual experience is at least as much personal as physical. If the Freudians are right, our whole unconscious selves are involved with our sexuality. Hence even to treat sex as an essentially emotional matter is too limiting. We are more than our feelings, no matter how ecstatic. We are not sensitive animals who are conscious of the joys of coupling, but persons, engaging in the most intimate act of human relationship regularly possible.

The most important part of the sexual act is what the partners mean to each other and what they are saying to each other in this unique way. Feelings are obviously involved. But to concentrate on my feelings or yours is to limit too severely what passes on the human level between two who make love out of love. Concern for the other as a whole person and not as a sexual partner, participation of the whole self and not just the mind trying to maximize the feelings, takes our intercourse from the animal level and makes it fully human. I know that we are not capable of such interchange and relationship constantly, but it can happen. And because it is so difficult to put into words, because it remains finally a mystery, is no reason to deny its reality or reject it as our ideal.

Something similar seems to characterize many Jews' approach to God. I doubt that they have read the great modern rationalistic critics of religion like Antony Flew among the British and Kai Nielsen among the Americans. Their approach to the reality of God owes less to analytic philosophy than to the sort of humanistic skepticism represented by Morris Raphael Cohen or Horace Kallen. Whatever their philosophical sources, such people are so dogmatic about what constitutes proper definitions, concepts, verifiability or the logic of religious language, that, by definition, it becomes impossible for anyone to experience transcendence. Before they can feel, they are questioning. Before they can encounter, they analyze. They are so ready to adopt the skeptical stance that they never engage whatever might stand before them.

For sexual intercourse to be human we must at some point go beyond the mind and its purposes and let the experience be what it is. So in trying to know God, once the intellect has done what it can to prepare us, we must move beyond it and let the religious experience occur as it will. Then, after the fact, we have a moral obligation to reflect cognitively upon what has happened to us and, in the new fullness of our being, determine what we must do. What troubles me is that just as rationalism applied to sex makes love impossible, so the secularist insistence upon skeptical intellectuality makes God unknowable—even if He is there.

These developments are culturally related. They are part of the process, as we have discussed before, of denying persons their fullness. I believe that Martin Buber was not only right but prophetic when he wrote *I and Thou* fifty years ago. If our whole society had a greater sense of what it means to be a person we would not have so much trouble knowing God. And if we were better at having real relationships with people we would find it rather natural to have, and know we have, a real relationship with God.

I think it is this sort of technical overemphasis on intellect that has kept many of us from facing up to what, I think, we believe. Ironically enough, it was the Jewish death-of-God movement, with its emphasis on the Holocaust, that raised the possibility that we had more faith than we had thought.

The argument against God seemed irrefutable. Any God who could permit the Holocaust, who could remain silent during it, who could "hide His face" while it dragged on, was not worth believing in. There might well be a limit to how much we could understand about Him, but Auschwitz demanded an unreasonable suspension of understanding. In the face of such great evil, God, the good and the powerful, was too inexplicable. So men said, "God is dead."

In Richard Rubenstein's version, the Holocaust had made clear that the universe stood empty of any meaning or value that transcended man. At its heart there was nothing, only the great tide of being that endlessly gave existence and just as inexorably swallowed it up in death. With that sensational announcement, everyone fully expected the Jewish community to respond eagerly to the new legitimation of atheism and agnosticism. Had not Jews for years claimed that they didn't believe, that their synagogue affiliation was really for the sake of their children or their parents? Had not the thoroughly secularized, university-trained, culturally astute Jewish sophisticates long insisted that religion was something only for the weak or the aged to take seriously? So when, about the same time, Sherwin Wine founded an atheist congregation and then found six other rabbis to join him in drawing up a platform of humanistic Judaism, it seemed that a new emancipation would dawn on the Jewish community. The old, hateful hypocrisy of the religion game could now be swept away, and the true attitude of the modern Jew could appear: We do not believe in God.

It never happened. Instead of Jews rallying to the standard of atheistic or agnostic Judaism, the movement died quickly in the Jewish community. Some rabbis are now able to say that they do not know whether God is real—some 17 percent of the Reform rabbinate—but otherwise, the death-of-God agitation is now only of academic interest, in the most invidious sense of that term. No one predicted or could have foreseen such an outcome. Analyzing its probable causes will, I believe, teach us much about ourselves.

For many people, of course, God had been dead or as good as dead for some time. To them, the announcement was old news. It was to the people still within the broad circumference of Jewish religiosity that the new atheism came as a surprise, for it was offered by men within the synagogue as a basis for creating a new style of religious existence. But it was these people, the ambivalent, the unsure, the now believing, now unbelieving masses, who themselves gave the answer to the call to thoroughgoing disbelief. We cannot point to any theoretician—say, an Elie Wiesel or an Emil Fackenheim—and say he explained how God could permit the Holocaust. The thinkers would say that this was never their intention. Rather, I think we must attribute the rejection of the Jewish death-of-God movement to the judgment of the masses of Jews themselves. To put what happened, as I see it, most concisely, the Jewish community was radicalized by the announcement that God had died. Only, instead of moving to the pole of atheism as it first seemed it would go, American Jewry moved, almost unwittingly, toward the pole of belief. I believe the reasoning behind that shift went something like this:

Despite the relativism that we had learned in the thirties from the anthropologists and psychologists, it was clear that the Nazis were unambiguously evil. They were masters of evil, for what they did was willed, deliberate, persistent and immoral, and in their efforts they were joined by many educated, enlightened men, fully conscious of what they were doing. Their barbarities so violated our deepest sense of what is good that if God did not act against the Nazis, He did not exist—He was dead.

But thought cannot stop there. Every assertion has its conseqences and the death of God had most peculiar ones. What does this new realism, that God is dead, teach us about Auschwitz? Why, simply that it is normal and not exceptional at all. The Holocaust was a revelation, not a calamity, for it was a direct reflection of the reality in the universe. As it is empty of meaning, or quality, and man is free to do what he wishes, so the Holocaust properly mirrors man's nature, one part of which is surely brutish and destructive. Indeed if the fundamental movement of creation is death-bringing, as Richard Rubenstein asserted, then the Holocaust is a triumphant image of reality.

We have no right, then, to complain about Auschwitz. It may be personally sobering, particularly if we had family there. It would obviously have been painful had it engulfed us. But this is as much negativity as is now appropriate. With God dead, Auschwitz has become a reasonable expectation and a far more logical sort of conduct than goodness, generosity, saintliness or messianic persistence in history. With the transcendent ground of our morality gone, evil has been domesticated among us, and righteousness has become a quirk, a whim, an abnormal assertion of the self against the nature of things.

At this point many Jews realized that the protests against God had gone too far. They could easily sympathize with a passion for justice and righteousness so great that one must challenge God Himself over them. Not only Job, but Abraham, Jeremiah and the Psalmists had all shown the Jewish legitimacy of such contention with God. But if the result of the new debate is that justice and righteousness are themselves negated, that they are no longer utterly significant to human existence, then we have gone too far. The very indignation and outrage that brought us to our great denial has become completely unreasonable. We have found an "explanation" for the Holocaust which turns out to be a contradiction of the pain and passion that made us demand an explanation in the first place. Job would be foolish to try to argue with a dead God.

The death of God turned out to mean the death of moral value—and most Jews would not accept that. But, in rejecting the death of God, a positive awareness could not help but dawn. While most Jews don't believe in very much, they also obviously don't believe in nothing. In contrast to the image of their pious grandfathers or by the saccharine standards of conventional American religiosity, they are gross disbelievers. But confronted with nihilism, with the belief that there is no standard of value at the heart of things, and seeing around them the growing evil effects of a value-free view of things, American Jews began to realize that there are some things they stand for and believe in.

I do not mean that many Jews now turned to God with a strong, conscious, discerning belief. We remain too solidly imbedded in the secularist twentieth century for that. But I do think that there is a new receptivity among us to the hidden depth of our belief and to the reality beyond it. And for some Jews this recognition has proceeded to the point where they acknowledge that their moral commitments do not ultimately arise from self or society but from a transcendent, commanding source. Thus their moral sensitivity and their sense of human values lead to a religious consciousness, and the sense of transcendence becomes a way of standing in the presence of God.

There is, of course, a great philosophical leap from a glimmering sense of transcendent morality to what Judaism calls God. God is, in most Jewish teaching, even today, concerned with more than ethics. But for Cohen and Kaplan, Buber and Rosenzweig, Heschel and other contemporary thinkers, He remains primarily the God of righteousness, and it is as the ground and guarantor of our highest values that modern Jews, despite all the barriers they have erected against experience of Him, have become open to Him. I know that some philosophers believe one does not need God for a transcendent ground of ethics, and for others the linguistic rules by which ethical thinking must be done would preclude God's being any such thing. Yet if ethics implies the sort of cosmic significance and messianic persistence that I have been talking about, I do not see any secular meta-ethics capable of grounding it.

Remember, I am presenting here not an argument that will force you to accept its conclusions—even logical coercion degrades people—but an explanation of what I believe has taken place in many a Jewish heart. I find it significant that when some few philosophers, like Henry Sidgwick or G. E. Moore, dare to go beyond utilitarian or naturalistic explanations of ethics, they speak of the ethical as a special sense in man or a self-justifying experience. To me, the implications of such uncommon philosophic assertions are quite clear. Were such philosophers not bound by the conventions of their guild, they would recognize that they were talking about something quite close to religious experience. Since my Jewish faith teaches that God stands in relationship with all men, I am not surprised that there is a universal possibility of reaching Him, particularly when what men then learn is how they ought to live.

I think this precarious path of inner analysis must be pursued one step further. The death-of-God movement opened some of us to our faith by the negative process of showing us that we do not completely disbelieve. We have also had a positive religious experience as well, but it has largely been repressed because we are so fully conditioned to skepticism. I am referring to what happened to many Jews during the Arab-Israeli Six-Day War of June, 1967.

Think back to your experience then, with as much freshness and immediacy as you can muster. For three weeks preceding the war there had been mounting tension in the Near East, climaxing in Arab threats to exterminate the Israelis. Once again the great powers did nothing to safeguard the State of Israel's rights, in this case, specifically, passage through the Straits of Tiran. They seemed quite content to let her fend for herself—that is, win or undergo a Holocaust. Through television, the world Jewish community became a personal part of these events. Having compulsively discussed the Hitler terror since the Eichmann trial, many a Jew could not help but ask, what will God do this time? In those grim Monday hours of the beginning of the war and the news blackout, God Himself seemed to be on trial. No one said it. Few could bring themselves to think it consciously, much less say it, but I doubt that many Jews did not harbor some such notion.

When the Israelis were saved, when victory came, and with such Biblical decisiveness, when Jerusalem was in Jewish hands and men who had never prayed before stood groping for words before The Wall, most Jews around the world, were, for a moment, conscious that something had "come to pass." Even as they were grateful to the Israeli army and full of praise for Dayan and Rabin, they felt a thankfulness to something that transcended even the most significant of men. They knew then that God had been good, that He was somehow present. It was, to be sure, a surfeit of emotion, an overflow of relief and elation. But the spirit reached out beyond exhilaration and enthusiasm to that which is the abiding source of goodness in all creation.

I think we experienced His presence then—and that it was no illusion. But it passed. Since then it has been entirely repressed. When, on occasion, I have discussed this Biblical moment I have met, at best, with indulgence for my softhearted, unrealistic temper. I may be wrong in my judgment of what occurred, but I do not propose to surrender it because the modern mind says it could not happen or is not comfortable with an erratic Divine Presence. Almost everyone has better and more numerous questions than I have answers, but I will not deny what was real and true to me, as best I can understand it, because I am not now able to explain just what God did, or how He did it, or why He was present in 1967 but not in 1944, or why He showed us His goodness this time and not His wrath. I believe that understanding must try to be true to what seems genuine experience. I believe that we must avoid denying such meaningful and coherent experience merely because our understanding cannot easily fit it into precise categories.

One argument must be faced, for it discovers an immoral element in my response. The charge is made that it is a vicious thing suddenly to find God in the defeat and death of one's enemies, particularly when one has not been able to find Him in much of the rest of contemporary experience. Such an experience is ethnocentrism projected into the heavens, an arrogant effort to make what is good for the Jews God.

The charges wound, and they may be true. Worse, there is no way to answer them. When it comes to motives, we must all be prepared to face the reality of the urge to evil in us and try to be open to the mixture of motives propelling us. But some things can be said. I saw and heard little rejoicing over the defeat of the Arabs and none at all at their death. The real joy came, quite simply, because there was no new Holocaust and Jerusalem was again ours. There was happiness that the Israelis had won, and that seems to bother many people. One gets the impression Jews are not supposed to be victorious, that it is un-Jewish to triumph. But a morality that permits only the other side to win is utterly spurious. Who else in all the world thinks that way? It can be nothing but self-hatred when Jews are afraid of what the Gentiles will say if we are too successful.

But it must be quickly added that Jews do not find God only in Jewish victories. Nothing could be clearer in Jewish literature than that He has most often been seen in disaster. From Nebuchadnezzar to Chmielnicki, prophets and chroniclers have regularly tried to read in their people's troubles God's judgment upon them. One special source of Jewish suffering in modern history is that men have been so bestial to us that we cannot connect their acts to our sins or God's judgment. His absence has left us feeling alone and isolated. This too is not unique. Not every catastrophe of Biblical times yielded a message concerning Him. Mostly, men do not see. Sometimes He is not there. Not every major event is a transcendental experience.

The same is true with Jewish triumphs. We have not always laid claim to seeing His hand in them. The most dramatic instances are surely those connected with the State of Israel. Almost no one said that God was visible in the 1957 Sinai campaign victory. Even the establishment of the State in 1948, though some people danced in the street and a few mystics spoke of the "beginnings of the redemption," produced no depth of response comparable to June 1967. This was a supreme experience.

When we deny its special character today, I feel that we say less about what happened than about the struggle inside us. The skeptical, secular, Marrano side of us is doing everything in its power to maintain its dominance. Were we to admit to ourselves that we have personally stood in His presence, we would be powerfully moved to throw off our Marrano guises and rework our lives in terms of Him and our relation to Him as part of the people of His Covenant. For in that June 1967 experience, momentary though it was, all the fragments of our existence finally came together. We could see that there was meaning to life and that we needed to struggle for it. We could understand why, in the midst of the brutalities of history, it was vital that we strive to be moral. We knew that this faith of ours—which is not shared by every man of modern culture and breeding—is a deep and abiding Jewish commitment. We realized how deeply we were tied to the Jewish people and its insistence on surviving history so as to bring the Messiah. We recognized that we were one with all the Jews of the world and all the Jews of history in a loyalty to what our God requires of mankind and, as a result, particularly requires of the Jewish people.

If ever understanding clashed with experience and failed, it was when we all—most of us by television—first stood at the Wall. Rationally, it would be difficult to think of a symbol less likely to move us. Most of us do not pray for the restoration of the Temple, and the idea of killing animals and splashing their blood against the altar is repulsive to us. The stones themselves are aesthetically uninteresting and historically insignificant—none of those visible comes from Solomon's original Temple or Haggai and Zechariah's second building. In fact, what we saw then was only the outer retaining wall holding up the extended Temple hill, not a wall of one of the sacred compounds or the Holy of Holies building. On every count the Wall should not have opened us to experience of the numinous. But it did.

Today it is another tourist attraction. But for a while it was holy ground, a sacred spot, a gate that opened to our past, our people and our God. For a moment it healed us and we were whole. If we would acknowledge this experience, if we would remember it, then it would become the model by which we could recognize that less overwhelmingly, in the still, small way in which significance infuses the everyday, such experiences of the reality of the Covenant are, or can become, a regular part of our lives.

I think the time is ripe for us to stop being Marranos and establish our Jewish integrity. That will come when we make the Covenant the basis of our existence, when we link our lives with our people, joining in its historic pact with God. This commitment focuses Jewishness in an act of self—not in ideas, or practice, or birth alone; but all of these now will take their significance from an utterly fundamental relationship of self with God and people. I do not know quite what forms of Jewishness this will lead to. I only know that if one cares, one must act. If we will to be Jews, if we make our Jewishness our means of facing existence, then every part of our lives will be Jewish. Since we are part of a historic tie, we will honor the tradition; and since we affirm this in our being, we will create and innovate so as to express it our way. One cannot know where such personalist covenanting may lead us. But I am less afraid of what we may choose in such Jewish integrity than that we will do nothing and by our indolence perpetuate our Marrano inauthenticity.

# CHAPTER 11

# The Existential Jew

Today mankind desperately needs people who are creatively alienated. To be satisfied in our situation is either to have bad values or to understand grossly what man can do. Simply to be opposed to "the system" leads to quixotic protests that work to entrench the established wrong and promote despair and passivity. Creative alienation implies sufficient withdrawal from our society to judge it critically, but also the will and flexibility to keep finding and trying ways of correcting it.

I think Jewishness offers a unique means of gaining and maintaining such creative alienation. This was not its primary role in the lives of our parents or grandparents. As immigrants or refugees, as the heirs of a painful history of being outsiders now suddenly ended, they wanted nothing more than identification with the majority. And for most contemporary American Jews, the sociological drift, acclimation to the society, remains the basic direction of their existence. For a good number, that comes from a fundamental lack of security in their status. For a larger group it is the result of moral sloth. And the pervasive amorality of a technological age is likely to increase the pressures for conformity to the accepted ways of unrighteousness in our society.

From the standpoint of simple realism, I do not see how these personal and social pressures can be resisted, redirected or overcome. I assume that being a Jew is not a matter of realism but of historically demonstrated idealism and presently unquenched hope. I want as many Jews as possible, seeing their condition and the condition of mankind, to take up the perennial challenge of Jewishness. I want them to make being a Jew a matter of conscious, determined will, and so give their Jewishness the possibility of transforming their lives, sanctifying our communities and affecting the world at large.

I think the time is ripe for some such movement of Jewish self-determination. We are beyond the Jewish negativism of a previous generation and aware of the need for firm roots for our lives. The promise and the problem of this hour is our ambivalence. Without it, there can be no openness to a life of greater integrity and moral depth. But as long as we remain suspended in our indecision as to where we truly stand, we have neither the naïve security Jews years ago had in liberalism, nor the power that might come from a wholehearted affirmation of our Jewishness.

Most of us live on an untidy mix of things that we care about and believe in. These tend to change as we grow and get to know ourselves better. This basic dynamism of self-awareness cannot be overestimated. But neither must we downgrade the elements of stability in the self. People rarely alter all that much. For most men the process of maturing is one of finding and refining certain core commitments around which they will shape their lives. This is what we mean by integrity. It encompasses all three levels that we have been discussing. Intellectually, it appears in the growing coherence of our thinking. Psychologically, it is evident in the way our drives and interests take on a happy singleness of direction. But most important of all—and generally the least talked about—integrity means the clarification of what we truly care about and the shaping of our acts to those ends. Thus it is not a rigid fixing of our character for all time, but only the development of such firm foundations of being that we may be relied upon to be true to them as life continues.

Such integrity of self is especially difficult to come by today. We have so little certainty. Our beliefs tend to be temporary and fleeting. So we give the bits and pieces of our devotion to this and that, for shorter or longer periods. But, because there is little that is basic and lasting in us, our lives periodically reveal their ultimate emptiness, and we must acknowledge that we are neither integrated nor whole. Fragmentation and insecurity are our most pervasive personal and social maladies today.

Our Jewishness could be an extraordinary personal resource in this situation. But we cannot gain its benefits as long as we do not make it central to our lives. This existentialist sense of Jewishness as a way of centering our commitments is quite at variance with our customary ways of thinking about it as either holding certain ideas or observing certain practices. Let me try to make it clearer by a negative example. Let us take a look at the way in which such Jewish concerns as we do have tend to function in our lives.

Even for most of us who try to make our Jewishness significant, it generally remains marginal to our existence. We remain, in effect, men who are occasionally Jewish, people in general who happen to have been born among the Jews. Our Jewishness is peripheral to our effective selves. Of course, the gap between the two often seems slight, for we connect being Jewish with our basic ethical commitments and social values. But let the demands of our Jewishness conflict with our general desires, and it is quickly revealed which group of concerns is more fundamental to our lives. For most of us there is quite a different response— almost, it seems, an instinctive one—to Wednesday golf and Wednesday Passover services, to the call to Little League and to

Bar Mitzvah classes. There, in the need to choose, we see what we truly care about and thus, so to speak, who we truly are.

If we want the creative alienation that Jewishness has so extraordinarily engendered and empowered, the question of its centrality to our being becomes critical. As long as it is marginal in us, its power to help us to transcend our situation and yet work to better it is vitiated. Its guidance then is always subordinated to our more central interests. What our Jewishness asks of us must always wait upon the judgment of the something else that we more dearly care about—comfort, security, success, respectability. If, then, we rely more fundamentally on what society says is smart or on some image of our self as socially acceptable, our lives will finally reflect the fragmentation of our contemporary society. And just such a yield of emptiness is what I see multiplying in our community as Jews learn to slough off or repress the remnants of the Jewish values they were trained to in their youth.

Thus, the need to choose who we will be is becoming more pressing. Hardly a day now passes but that such maturity as we have won is not unexpectedly shaken by a new and realistic possibility in money, sex, drugs or power. We quake because we suddenly realize how much that we once decided was forbidden to us now appeals to us mightily. Often, we now realize, our apparent security in our present standards was born more out of prudence than out of our sense of what is ultimately valuable in life. Now we see that with a little effort of will and intelligence we might have new thrills without great payment, that what once seemed to have a high risk or be taboo is only another way to live. This experience is called temptation. It shakes us because we find that we are not as sure as we thought we were of our most cherished values. The problem is not that we believe in nothing but that we do not really know what we care about most of all. The result is that we, and our civilization as well, are suffering from a lack of integrity about humane existence.

There is a virtue in temptation. It forces us to choose between competing values, to assess who we are and assert what we most truly care about. Since most of us do not know this or cannot bring ourselves to limit our identity—to say I am this and not that, however seductive the "that" may seem—this ambivalence often leads to some sort of personal collapse. A good many of the tragedies we see among young people have come from not having values secure enough to enable them to live with the freedom our society gives them. I think the same is true of many adults, only, because they have waited longer to try certain options, they are better at covering up their inability to cope with the human results. The results are in some ways more tragic. Youth still has the time and energy to recoup. Adults often destroy the integrity of a life by a shift in their values.

If we would decide to move our Jewish faith and belief from the margin to the very center of our effective being, if we willed to pivot our lives about the Jewish ethos we now only peripherally use, we might hope to surmount the crisis of our civilization. I certainly do not mean that such fundamental Jewishness of self would make us strangers to the anxieties of freedom or the perils of temptation. I only mean we would have an unusually valuable help in maintaining an honorable integrity in our existence. I do not think that one decision will free us of the troubles of our time. Such a Jewish stance toward life is not won once and forever by most of us. It is continually tested by life and thus needs continual reassertion. This is where customs and community and tradition play their powerful stabilizing roles.

This hard-core Jewishness is not being suggested as an infallible answer to all questions. It does not make plain how to pacify Red China or depollute Lake Erie. It only helps you know who you are and are becoming. It gives you a growing sense of what you must do if you would be true to yourself. Not to do some things, or to agree to do others, would be to violate myself. I know that, so no one compels me in my decisions. I compel myself—at the risk of losing or gaining myself. It is a new sense of commandment, personally imposed but transcendently grounded.

The Jewish health I am looking for is founded on the rejection of any inner split between self and Jew. It bases itself on our effort to be, at our very roots, Jew and person all at once. We now want to build our existence in such a way that there is regularly no place in the growing integrity of our being where we are not Jews. This is the only authentic response to the old question of what is Jewish about us. Now we will be entirely Jewish. To the observer it may seem as if our acts are only what men of other faiths or similar values perform. Yet, since these universal, humane activities arise in us because of our Jewish commitments, our fight against air pollution and world hunger will be as fully Jewish as our protests against Russian anti-Semitism or our concern with Israeli archaeology. And if such achieved centering and integration of self is more than we can manage at the moment, then the very act of determining to achieve it will be the beginning of our healing. Being on the way is already decisive for ourselves and for humanity.

# CHAPTER 12

# Updating an Argument: American Jewry Faces The 1980's

*The Mask Jews Wear* sought to transform American Jewish self-consciousness in two major respects. First, it hoped to persuade all those American Jews who thought of their Jewishness as essentially a commitment to ethics — and hence a universal human concern — to acknowledge how deeply ethnic their personal roots were. (Chapters 1-6.) Second, it argued that even the richest form of secular Jewishness would not meet our needs for a compelling form of ethnic identity or be true to our deepest intuitions of what it means to be a Jew. We are, I contended, less agnostic and more believing than we thought ourselves to be. Our immediate Jewish task, then, was to reappropriate a personal relationship with God and thereby be able to reassert our people's historic Covenant with God (Chapters 7-11.)

Looking back now on the 1970's — the book appeared several weeks before the 1973 Israeli Yom Kippur War — I see much in American Jewish experience which has confirmed these theses. The first, the shift to ethnicity, has become virtually a truism of our contemporary community life though in a fashion that has created new problems for us. The second, the turn to spirituality, has to my happy surprise become the major motif of the Jewish life of an increasing minority in our community. It has demonstrated a vigor and staying power that were totally unimaginable as we entered the 1970's. Both phenomena will be critical to Jewish existence in the 1980's.

Like most Americans in the 1970's, Jews lost their old confidence in liberal democracy and often instead asserted their ethnic self-interest. Through the decade we were obsessed by a fear for Jewish survival. At home most Jews were far from learned, observant or pious. About 40 per cent of the marriages involving a Jew were with non-Jewish partners (though many of these were second or later marriages). Our lovers of the State of Israel did not learn Hebrew and our appreciators of eastern European Jewish culture did not speak Yiddish much. Jewish religiosity also seemed a veneer, rarely going beyond a few rituals and an occasional synagogue visit. Inflation and aging badly hurt our expensively budgeted, child-centered synagogues.

Internationally, our fears were centered on the threats to the existence of the State of Israel. For almost every Jew, it symbolizes the Jewish will to live despite the Holocaust. Its continued existence is therefore a human and Jewish testimony of metaphysical import. So to see the Israelis cruelly isolated in international affairs, while gun-toting terrorists were welcomed to the rostrum of the United Nations and the barely healed survivors of the Holocaust were termed racists, brought most Jews to insist that nothing should take precedence over our devotion to Jewish survival and thus to the State of Israel. Our activism on behalf of the Soviet Jews derived from this same concern.

The Yom Kippur War showed that one substantial Israeli blunder might lead to the destruction of the State of Israel. Until Camp David, our community lived with a constant sense of threat.

Before that and in different ways since, the American pressures on the Israelis to settle with the Egyptians as the United States thought proper brought most of our leadership and much of our community to the brink of panic. We discovered political and religious zealots among us. Though a small number in our community, they have occasionally been able to carry the majority along with them. At the other extreme and on the far horizon there is the possibility that a functioning Israeli-Egyptian peace treaty would end the emergency mentality that has energized our community for over a decade. In any case, we know that nothing going on among us arouses our Jewish loyalties as deeply as does any peril to the State of Israel.

As we enter the 1980's, then, almost everything significant about contemporary Jewish life is based on our passionate ethnicity with its focus on the State of Israel.

An important consequence of this is the low-level tension which has arisen between synagogues and federations. In the late 1960's, as a result of the Jewish move to the suburbs, synagogues became the central institution of American Jewry. Today, they must, at the least, share power with federations which are the instrumentality through which our relation to the State of Israel is most directly expressed, that is, by sending it philanthropic funds. (The socioeconomic factor is also significant. Federation leadership is largely a matter of one's ability to give. In federations and the national Council of Federations Jews of means and influence can meet their peers. Thus, today, it is primarily in the federations, not the synagogues, that what normally passes for American Jewish power is structured.)

The Israelocentricity of the federations' fundraising has had an unexpected effect. A generation or so back, their focus was largely local and national charities, and their leadership was regularly accused of "not being very Jewish." The classic charge was that they gave millions for Jewish hospitals which sometimes had no kosher kitchens for observant Jews, while giving little to Jewish education. In the past decade, federations have "Judaized." Practically, if they do not assure Jewish survival, they will soon have no donors. Idealistically, the issue of Jewish survival has gotten them involved in the intensification of Jewish life, including the funding of Jewish day schools, once considered an "un-American" activity. Nearly one third of all children receiving a Jewish education currently are in such programs (for which busing and the deterioration of public education are only partial explanations). As successive Israeli emergencies have brought American Jews to give more, local Jewish activities have benefited in the process. While synagogues have been tight for funds, federations have, relatively speaking, had money for Jewish programming.

But once federations move on from fundraising to sponsoring Jewish activities, they easily run into conflict with synagogues, which are not without considerable power. In the past few years American Jewish religious life has recovered from the numerical and financial low period of the early 1970's. Despite our continuing zero population growth and our relative suburban stability, there has been some gain in synagogue formation. A threatened oversupply of rabbis has not developed. This growth has occurred in the face of a small but steady stream of synagogue mergers in small towns and changing neighborhoods, a process aided by the practical disappearance of practical differences between most Jews regardless of denominational labels. Only a minority among us takes ideology seriously. Mostly we divide between those who prefer more tradition in their lives and those who prefer less — but almost all of us are determined to make up our own minds as to just what we propose to do as Jews. This vulgarization of the Reform principle of personal autonomy is that standard by which most American Jews, in fact, conduct their Jewish lives — but of this more later.

The potential for conflict between federations and synagogues seems unlikely to lead to major difficulty. Neither institution can easily do without the other; the leaders of neither group seem interested in a power-grab or fight. Until now, the Israeli peril made it necessary for both sides to subordinate their immediate interests to the general good. A lessening of tensions in the Middle East or, more likely, the continuing American economic pinch, may result in a relative decline in gifts to federations, thus cramping such expansionism as they demonstrate.

One major outcome of the new ethnicity was not obvious to me when I wrote this book. It has led many Jews to abandon much of that commitment to universal ethics which has for some time been the average American Jew's understanding of the essence of Judaism. I should have been more observant, that is, more politically than ideologically oriented. In the mid-1960's Lyndon Johnson had told our leaders that the Israelis would get no Phantom jets until American Jews stopped pressuring the United States to get out of the Vietnam War. From that time on, and decisively in the 1970's, our community has been increasingly docile on the ethical questions facing our nation and the world.

Nationally, we used to be among the most avid supporters of civil rights for all, even despised minorities. Now our community leaders are worried lest they be indicted as insufficiently militant on behalf of Jewish rights, thus repeating the errors of the Holocaust. When 20 some American style Nazis wanted to march in Skokie, Ill., American Jewry was alarmed and the defense of the Nazis by the American Civil Liberties Union led to numerous Jewish resignations from that organization. Since we are discouraged about what we can do to improve our society and we are not clear how much other Americans are willing or capable of extending democracy, we devote our energies largely to the survival of our people.

Internationally, we give ourselves almost exclusively to the problems of the State of Israel and Soviety Jewry. Only occasionally are Jewish groups concerned with world hunger, disarmament or universal human rights. The United Nations offers a telling instance. We once supported it enthusiastically. After seeing it honor Yasir Arafat we are cynical about the authenticity of its commitment to world peace and human solidarity.

Perhaps it is unfair to link the issues but the Jewish turn from universal ethics has been accompanied by a shift from liberal political concerns, previously the means by which we thought to put our ethics into action. Our current indifference to most social ethical causes is undoubtedly a reaction to our previous euphoria about the possibilities of political ethicism. We believed that through government we could bring the Messianic Age — and what we got was the 1970's, that is, a threat of social collapse and not utopia.

The hardest thing to face during the past decade has been the way in which the universal ethical programs often seemed to run counter to our Jewish group interests. Socially, we are no longer among the underprivileged but either one of the most or the most successful religio-ethnic group in America. We attained this high status in the present social order. Any proposed change in it — say, affirmative action at universities — immediately affects our status and privileges.

The old notion that Jews should take short-term ethnic losses to achieve long-range democracy seems naive. We cannot honestly believe that ethical political action, pursued in the face of ethnic sacrifice, will create so good a society that people will stop being anti-Semitic.

In world affairs, our political situation is starkly ethnocentric. The State of Israel needs American Jews as its lobby for a high United States defense budget, an anti-Soviet foreign policy, little aid to Arab countries and much aid to the Israelis. They are not interested in our devoting such political clout as we have to improving American democracy, particularly when that may tend to alienate the established American power interests. Zionism once meant an opportunity to show the world what Jewish and hence humane politics might be. I think it fair to say that supporting Israeli political objectives has often meant damping one's ethical liberalism.

This is a most troublesome issue. Fortunately, on many levels it simply dissolves because we know that nothing so well exemplifies the Jewish will to live and to do so with quality as does the State of Israel. Thinking of its accomplishments, despite its crushing burdens, we may take great ethical encouragement from what even Jewish secularity, as exemplified by the Israelis, retains of a Jewish sense of desirable human existence. Nonetheless, something has changed. At one time it looked as if the politics connected with the State of Israel would be positive, ethical, humanistic and universal. That is no longer the rule.

Obviously, there are many other facets to our current diminution of general ethical concern, particularly our changed view of human-kind and its capacity to do evil. We cannot go back — I hope we do not want to go back — to the idea that being ethical is the essence of being Jewish. I had argued against such a position as the first major thesis of this book. I tried to show that our Jewish ethics needs its ethnic base. But we have moved to a more tribal stance than I had imagined we would or that our heritage would justify. In the present situtation I deem it important to assert the converse of my previous principle: Jewish ethnicity without Jewish ethics is unworthy of our tradition. Permit me, therefore, to state three theses on the continuing significance of universal ethics to Judaism.

The first of these is the primacy of ethics in Jewish duty. This is not the same as saying that ethics is the essence of Judaism, though it is surely related to that assertion. I am only pointing out that nothing is a more significant test of the "good Jew" than ethical behavior. That may not be all a good Jew has to do, but is the least one expects. No amount of other Jewish observance should substitute for a refusal to do the moral act we are capable of. I am convinced most American Jews still believe that, though few now speak of it. I take as my evidence the almost universal revulsion felt in the Jewish community at Bernard Bergman's role in the New York nursing home scandal.

Second, I contend that our involvement in the general concerns of our society must be a significant aspect of our present Jewish prac-tice. Had many people in western civilization not come to think universally about human responsibility, we Jews would still be in the ghetto or worse. Intellectually, the notion of universal ethical duties is the foundation of the emancipation of the Jews and the basis of our right to participate as equals in general society. Unless we affirm such an ethic, we deny the grounds of our unimpeded participation in western civilization and the basis upon which we assert that our emancipation needs yet to be fully completed.

I did not see that this classic liberal assertion has been invalidated by the Holocaust. Though the Nazi brutality may teach us a new and bitter realism about human nature, we and all moral people are repelled by it as the antithesis of our faith that no group is an exception to the mandates of justice and mercy. Our moral outrage at the Nazis is premised upon our insistence that they knew what acts human beings ought never to do. They were guilty, despite all social pressure, only because there is a universal morality all peoples can know and follow. Shall Jews, who have suffered so much from the particularism of other peoples, now fail to give appropriate devotion to our duties to all of humankind?

Practically, too, it ill behooves a people obsessed about its survival to as good as deny its responsibilities to its society. What moral judgement must be made of an ethnic group which has benefitted extraordinarily from participating in the general community — as a result of its hard work, to be sure — now refusing to give back to that community a significant measure of its interest and energy? Most Jews who advocate a minimal involvement in general social affairs refuse to speak of it openly, for they know it would be self-incriminating. Such closet ethnocentrism has become widespread in the Jewish community with deleterious effects on Jewish character.

Third, I continue to affirm the thesis that political activism is, in our time and place, a valuable way to create righteousness. Traditional Jewish law doesn't call for civic involvement, but for emancipated Jews to utilize their social franchise to bring greater social justice into being seems to be an obvious extension of classic Jewish duty. Its clear-cut model is Zionism. The State of Israel does not exist because of traditional Jewish law. For Orthodoxy, Zionism was long a heretical assumption of the Messiah's prerogative and an interference with God's providence. The notion that people ought to be politically active is a modernist ideal we Jews learned from western democracy, not from the Torah. As a result of it, not only were we emancipated in Europe but we finally learned to emancipate ourselves. I do not see how modern Jews can turn their backs on politics as a significant means of effectuating Jewish ethical ideals.

If we acknowledge the truth of these three premises, we could restore a proper balance between our ethical and our ethnic commitments as Jews, the sort of proper dialectic between Jewish universalism and particularism I argued for in the early chapters of this book. That brings me to my second major theme, that the rich Jewishness of balanced human and folk concern makes sense only when self-consciously based on religious belief.

Many American Jews have come to share that understanding, a phenomenon almost totally inconceivable when the 1970's began. Then we were at the height of the death-of-God debate and the only question seemed to be the form of nonbelief our emerging Judaism would soon take. To understand what has happened in the intervening decade we must keep in mind that, unlike Jews of some years previous, we did not think of ourselves as atheists. The Jewish socialists and intellectuals of yesterday and their Zionist counterparts were certain there was no God. Marx had shown that religion was a device used by the upper classes to screen their exploitation and Freud had exposed the infantile fantasies that gave it credence. Morever, science dictated atheism. To many a Jew these voices were the modern equivalent of Sinai.

Yet atheism seemed an overstatement to most contemporary Jews. It knew too much and its assertive negativity showed that its adherents were still hung up on God. Agnosticism provided us with a cleaner resolution of the Oedipal project. One no longer sullied

oneself attacking traditional belief. Rather, one withdrew to the ir-
reproachable perspective of awaiting more data. Surely reasonable
people could not be expected to act upon what they were not sure of.
One therefore felt quite justified in setting aside the question of
God, ostensibly until proof was forthcoming. In fact, we set such
high standards of skepticism in the face of possible proofs that the
theistic burden of argument was impossible to bear. The guilt
associated with this stance was easily offset by the sense of
righteousness connected with the label of agnostic. Against the
believers and the atheists, one was a true intellectual, open-minded
and searching, not closed and dogmatic. We flattered ourselves that
we were always open to new evidence. Privately we knew, having
studied anthropology and read Dostoevski, that no one was likely to
be able to demonstrate to us that there was a God.

As it turned out, our self-satisfaction with our agnosticism was
based on an assumption: one didn't need religious faith to ground a
strong sense of ethics or a commitment to high human standards.
Some of us based our sense of values on science, more on the social
sciences, particularly psychology; others counted on the ennobling
influences of literature and the arts, the democratic process or
simply the innate goodness of people. In one's everyday life one saw
decent folk who professed no religious faith — the Abraham Lincoln model — while one always knew or suspected that there were
scoundrels observant of the Torah (to borrow Nahmanides' phrase).
I think it remains true today that in a society permeated by the Bible
as ours was, biblical values would seem to be self-substantiating for
some time after the faith that gave rise to them had atrophied.

The realism engendered by our recent historical experience has
destroyed our naive confidence in the naturalness of values. The institutions we once counted on to produce the lifestyles we cherish,
will at best carry the sense of goodness we bring to them, but seem
more likely to distort if not pervert it. Neither the university nor the
theater nor the art gallery nor the mental health clinic nor the com-
municating family nor the latest techniques in self-realization, from

yoga to bio-feedback, explain why we should care passionately about being a certain kind of person, devoting ourselves to building loving patterns of family relationships and disciplining ourselves to try to create better communities and a more humane society. Reasonably intelligent people today accept all sorts of other possible life goals. What we once thought were human necessities now seem to the contemporary temper only alternative life styles. R.D. Laing declares schizophrenia a reasonable way of responding to our world and Sylvia Plath has become our symbol of facing life by committing suicide. Nihilism seems to have as much to commend it as ethics, though cultural lag requires that most of us practice prudence.

We never imagined that agnosticism might lead to the death of values. We always took it for granted that in a personal or social crisis our kind of agnostic would be learned, cultured, sensitive, liberal and dependable, in short not a bad sort of Jew to have around. Only now it appears that not having some sort of belief results in lacking strong conviction about why one should do this or not do that. In the current collapse of the virtue of secular culture, we are left with only our arbitrary choice as the ground for staking one's life on one's values. Character then becomes a whim and integrity is likely to be more an accident than moral accomplishment — and that is too much for most of us to abide. A universe empty of God is now suddenly devoid of any independent standard of value. In such a situation one has as much right to be a Nazi as a Jew — a blasphemy even our agnostic Jewish belief will not tolerate. We could live without God but not without our root sense that high human endeavor is a matter of cosmic significance.

In some such way, a new understanding dawned among us. We may believe little but we do not believe nothing. When we see those around us who do, apparently, believe in nothing and are, as a result, capable of doing anything, we recognize that we are not similarly empty of faith and affirmation. In the face of nihilism, I am arguing, Jews have been radicalized from their agnosticism. Affirming our values, we come in touch with a place deep within us where, despite all our doubts, we brush up against what our forebears called God.

Through this experience or something like it, a sizable minority in the Jewish community has discovered a transcendent dimension to existence. The Jewish spirit today in some small way is moving back to God. Astonishingly, we are seeing a direct spirituality being reborn among us. The Covenant, our ancient partnership, is newly alive in our fresh perception of the Other who meets and helps and commands and judges and forgives and saves and vindicates.

That does not mean that these newly believing Jews understand God or God's ways in history. The Holocaust remains as throbbing scar tissue. It does not mean that they know exactly what forms of Jewish duty properly express their responsibility under the Covenant. But in the midst of our secularized and troubled community, they recognize that the heritage of 4,000 years of Jewish experience remains the most valuable spiritual guidance available to them. In their search for closeness to God, they testify that this generation of Jews, as did the generations before them, has taken up and affirmed the Covenant as the basis of its existence. And in this surprising development they demonstrate to me that God, once again, has not let this people go. In our secularization, as ages ago in our slavery or our monarchy, God, too, has affirmed the Covenant with the Jewish people, again calling it, sending it and, I devoutly pray, protecting it against all enemies.

One sign of this religious renewal is seen in the shift of tone in our theological discussions. We still inquire where God was during the Holocaust but we have run out of fresh ways to ask the question or to explore possible answers to it. The topic is more a duty than a living challenge — something we know we must keep ever present but that we have not yet been able to make part of our sanctifying rituals. The pressing theological questions now come from wondering how, as individuals or a community, we can survive this age of pervasive uncertainty.

A major response to this inquiry is found in the emergence among us of a small but vigorous believing modern Orthodoxy. It holds faithful observance of the Torah to be the necessary antidote to the pathology of modern civilization yet it is secure enough in its Jewishness to accept whatever in our culture seems humanly beneficial and does not conflict with the content or the tone of Jewish tradition.

This too must be considered one of the surprises of the 1970's, though its promise was far more evident a decade ago than was the abandonment of agnosticism among our liberals. During most of the emancipation process, modernity appeared to mandate the abandonment of traditional Jewish belief and practice. Jewish observance was burdensome for those adapting to the style of general society. Remaining distinctive seemed foolish when non-Jews turned out to be decent and western civilization's understanding of the universe seemed far more comprehensive and demonstrable than that of the Torah. All this was so widely assumed to be the necessary pattern of Jewish life in modern times that there was serious speculation as to how long Orthodoxy would survive.

One reason for the upsurge of Orthodoxy in the 1970's was the acculturation and economic maturation of the survivors of the Holocaust who had immigrated to the United States after World War II. Sizable numbers were observant Jews. After what they had been through, many had no interest in compromising their Judaism to make themselves more acceptable to the gentile world. Their presence had the effect of encouraging those elements in American Orthodoxy who had been fighting the adjustment psychology within their own movement. (The symbolic battleground of the fight for a genuine Orthodoxy was the issue of the mixed seating of men and women at synagogue services.)

What has made revitalized Orthodoxy so exciting to observers is that it is largely a movement of native not immigrant Americans. In our time, birth here and thorough acculturation has not meant becoming liberal in religion. To the contrary, we often see former liberals deliberately choose to be Orthodox. To them this is the selection of a life style which they believe will be best for them and their children.

The most powerful motive for affirming Orthodoxy is the revulsion many Jews have come to feel toward western civilization. Instead of being eager to be fully at home in and accepted by it, as were previous generations of modern Jews, they are repelled by its amorality and therefore desirous of maintaining some distance from it. When this motivation becomes intense, it leads such Jews to migrate to the State of Israel; at its height, they adopt a Hasidic or other European oriented Jewish life-style, though that is a rather uncommon choice.

At one time Conservative Judaism might have commended itself as offering a proper balance between a tradition which separated one from society and an adjustment which accepted its mores. For many American Jews it still fulfills that role. For others, it does not seem to take its commitment to Judaism seriously enough for it seems to make too few Jewish demands. Put more positively, many people who now propose to live as serious Jews wish to do so in as authentic a fashion as possible. For them that means Orthodoxy. This criticism of the Conservative movement from the right has largely been responsible for the traditionalist wing in the Conservative movement insisting that there has been too much change in recent years and not enough insistence upon proper Jewish legal discipline.

Two other factors have also contributed to the rise of the new Orthodoxy. One is the maturation of the relatively large number of students who attended Jewish all-day schools. They have the learning and skills which enable them easily to undertake living under the law and they were often exposed in their youth to the Orthodox role-models which they can now adapt to their own temperaments.

Credit must also be given to the maturation in America of what has been called "modern Orthodoxy." It represents a fusion between classic, *halachic* Judaism and American culture, as typified by Yeshiva University. This Orthodoxy does not equate authenticity with a return to the ghetto. It sees no good Jewish reason to sacrifice those accomplishments of western civilization which enrich Jewish lives while being compatible with traditional Judaism. It has established a pattern of American Jewish living which does not compromise with Jewish discipline, e.g. *mikvah*, the ritual bath required of women, yet allows for appropriate modern activities, e.g. *yeshivah* sports activities.

For all these reasons, Orthodoxy became in the 1970's a living option for Jews seeking to find a substantial role for Judaism in their lives. Most American Jews, however, have not taken that path. Despite some withdrawal from western culture and greater reverence for Jewish tradition, they remain determinedly non-Orthodox, that is, liberal Jews. Three groups of them may usefully be identified.

The first of these remains at the margins of serious Jewish commitment. They are Jews whose non-observance and general Jewish unconcern derive from their satisfaction with the older accommodationist strategy of modernizing Jewry. They have not felt the pain of the postmodern situation in which many Jews (and Christians) now find themselves. Some are more sophisticated than that but, recognizing the problems our new realism would bring them, maintain the illusion that western civilization remains fundamentally humanistic and a proper surrogate for Torah.

A second group — the mass of Jews, I think — flits uneasily between assimilation and ethnic affirmation. Oscillating between inner — and other-directedness keeps them ill-at-ease. They liked having Jewish spirituality directed into western civilization. They were raised in that style of Jewishness and are good at practicing it. Only many of them now realize that the rationale for such an existence has largely ended. Ideology once validated what sociology mandated and Jews lived in the faith that western culture was in itself spiritual. Today, striving to show one belongs is a goal unworthy of life's major devotion. The old American Jewish way no longer carries conviction, but many Jews cannot bring themselves to turn back to their heritage for serious guidance. They participate in what is currently fashionable as if it were still worth the stake of one's life, but quietly knowing it is not, they often find themselves dejected. If the future does not hold the sort of Israeli and Soviet Jewish emergencies which galvanized them into action in the 1970's, their long-range involvement in Jewish life is problematic.

The third group is that minority which has become engaged in the search for a newly serious Jewish identity but which cannot honestly be Orthodox. These Jews cannot automatically accept the traditional determination of Jewish duty. They want to make Judaism the basis of their personal existence and they know this means a commitment to some standard of Jewish discipline. They are too spiritually syncretistic to be Orthodox and too ritualistic and tradition-minded to follow the old liberal patterns. The classic expression of their neo-traditionalism is the several volume work, *The Jewish Catalog*. Though it is a comprehensive, detailed effort to reclaim as much of Jewish law and custom as possible, it sold over several hundred thousand copies. Its utterly unprecedented reception, together with the rise of the *havurah* movement, the face-to-face Jewish exploration groups, was the major internal community cultural phenomenon of the decade — and the two developments are not unrelated.

In substance, *The Jewish Catalog* appears to be a work of traditional Judaism. It revels in justifying those aspects of Jewish life which liberals had dismissed as unacceptable to the modern temper, for example, mysticism, or women's observance of the rites of the *mikvah*, the ritual bath. But in form, though this was surely unconscious, the work is radically unOrthodox. It proclaims itself to be a *Catalog*. Such a book is a compilation of resources one draws on to meet one's needs. One is pleased to find it rich with suggestions for that expands one's horizons. Its pages will open new possibilities of Jewish action and unanticipated ways in which one's Jewish identity may express itself. It leaves one free to select what one believes will be most valuable to oneself. It may try to entice; it never commands — and that marks its rejection of Jewish Orthodoxy. Its authors knew they would not be accepted by their readers if they presumed to tell them what they must do. They could not set before the reader a contemporary exposition of required behavior, what another generation could call *Shulchan Aruch,* a "Set Table."

These "new Jews", for all their postmodern interest in making Judaism the foundation of their lives, remain dedicated to the basic ethical axiom of modernity: people should have the right to choose for themselves how they ought to live. Autonomy, literally, "the self as the maker of its own laws," is the critical difference between liberal and Orthodox Judaism. For all its possible dangers, they believe that the modern emphasis on personal freedom and the right to make one's own decisions has given people a personal worth and dignity that cannot otherwise be obtained. If anything, the truth seems to them to be that, by taking their right of personal conscience and choice seriously, they are enabled to accept our heritage with new respect because they now need not fear it will tyrannize them. If they adopt this or that custom, use more Hebrew in prayer or are more visibly Jewish in their observance, that represents no return to Judaism as essentially external discipline or the acceptance of the contemporary Orthodox sages. They have rushed from secularism to Orthodoxy but are only redirecting the primary focus of their autonomy from the resources of general culture to the wisdom of our tradition.

The status of women in Jewish law has become a major symbol of the differences between Orthodox and liberal Jewish efforts to serve God under the Covenant. It arouses such passion that disputants often forget it is only one instance of the many problems modern Jews find with traditional Jewish law and faith. Rather than add another exposition to this voluminous literature, let me make my point here by a note on a procedural implication of the changes concerning women. Insofar as it has happened, how did women win some rights in modern Orthodoxy, most notably, that of receiving a full-scale Jewish education? Surely it came about as an unacknowledged response to the liberals' previous insistence, in a break with traditional Jewish practice, that women should be as fully educated as men. I suggest that this is but one of many examples of what an orthodoxy first proclaims as alien and heretical later being accepted and finally claimed to be what it had wanted all along. Contemporary Orthodoxy has drawn a line at counting women in the *minyan,* giving them an *aliyah* or granting them ordination as rabbis. Nonetheless, its women today attend the university, work away from their homes, even spending much of their time among gentiles, all acts unthinkable for the pious not so long ago. When liberal Jews view the slow and grudging but definite shifts in Orthodoxy's image of a pious Jewish woman, they are confirmed in their belief in the humanness of Jewish legal development. To them, the evolution of Jewish law owes more to the universal patterns of human social change than to God's determination that in Judaism the sexes will be legally separate though spiritually equal.

The Orthodox do not deny that the law is substantially human and that some of its difficulties are common to all religio-legal institutions. For their part, many liberals will agree that Jewish law is not merely human convention but reflects the inspired sense of what our people has come to know God wants of it. What is at stake between the two positions is not an exclusively human or Divine origin of the Torah but the balance between the two partners who determine it. Orthodoxy teaches that, for all its humanity, God established the law in its details and in its method of modification. Hence the human role in it is substantially subordinated to the Divine. Liberals see Jewish law, for all its reflection of the Divine, as an exercise in human spiritual creativity. That comes through to them not only in its content but even more clearly in the patterns of its historical development. To liberals, this fits in well with what they know about psychology and social process. These substantially explain not only much of the operation of Jewish law but the transcendent theological claims the Orthodox make for it. Knowing our tradition's human origins, the liberals feel enabled to accept its faults without defensiveness, to change them with sensitivity and to glory in the Jewish heritage's rare human accomplishment in so responding to God's commanding presence over the millenia.

I have often used the term Covenant to describe this neo-liberal/neo-traditional sort of relationship between our people and God. It has good Jewish warrant. Our Torah makes the astonishing assertion that the one God of all the universe enters into intimate relationships with all humankind. It was an extraordinary sort of partnership, considering the unequal capacity of the two allies. For the Children of Noah as well as the Children of Israel, the Torah utilized the term largely in the sense of legal contracts. The partners were then bound by the laws stipulated in their agreement. In our modern sense of Covenant, we shall want to stress the living relationship between the partners and see whatever we can then call "law" as the sense of duty, individual and communcal, that emerges from it. Judaism, understood today as Covenant, is the living, changing, dynamic interaction between the people of Israel through its individual members, and the transcendent realm of reality. This places far more trust in human power than does Orthodoxy but gives far more place to God than did classic religious liberalism.

In the usage, the word Covenant defines the meta-*halachic* basis of Judaism, that is, what Orthodox and non-Orthodox Jews fundamentally share. They stand in the same relationship with God, that is, the Covenant, they have a different understanding of the specific responsibilities which arise from it. For Orthodoxy, the law and the proper means of its interpretation are God-given. For liberalism, the law is created by the people of Israel as a result of standing in Covenant with God. For them, the Jewish tradition is essentially a human invention. This is saved from simple humanism because the tradition arises not out of the people's sense of self but from its recognition that is bound to God. It seeks to be true to itself by doing God's will as best the people of Israel can understand it. In this construction of chosenness, then, people play a self-determining, autonomous role; they are their own lawmakers. They are also God's partners as part of the Household of Israel's historic devotion to the Covenant. Hence their freedom is conditioned by God's reality and Jewish community and tradition, a situation which makes spiritual anarchy hardly conceivable and an eccentric Jewish practice unlikely.

Living our lives as Jews under the Covenant would reorient our understanding and practice of Judaism. Our peoplehood could be affirmed in joyful self-acceptance but the glory of its culture would now be seen in terms of its continuing response to God. Our humanity and our ethnicity would have to stand in judgment before our depth perception of the value inherent in the universe. What is "good for the Jews;" whether in the United States or in the State of Israel, would be ineradicably tied up with what is good in itself. Ethics would be that basic to Jewish existence.

Similarly, Torah would now be seen as a dynamic sense of responsibility. When it seems clear, after conscientious search, that our old forms no longer reflect our immediate Jewish sense of what God wants of us, then they not only may, but must, be changed. We liberals will therefore count women in the *minyan,* call them for *aliyot* and ordain them as rabbis in full authenticity to the Covenant. With our faith, to do anything less than that, indeed even to delay implementing such changes, would be sinful. That does not mean that every contemporary folk pattern should be given the status of a commandment. Our people prefer the *oneg shabat* to liturgy; they want public honor and communal power for giving *tzedakah;* and will do almost anything but serious Jewish study. Many of the actual folkways of American Jewry are a mockery of traditional Jewish ideals. We shall better be able to discern our people's triumphs from its failings if we remember it is called upon by its Covenant relationship to be holy.

For many people this sort of thinking about our Jewish religious responsibilities, now modern, now traditional, will prove difficult more by its form than its substance. All of us prefer a simple either/or to the complexities of a dialectic in which one belief is always held in tension with another. The times leave us little choice. As we enter the 1980's, many of us who have lived in the world of Jewish modernity can no longer be satisfied with a choice between supernaturalistic Orthodoxy and humanistic religious liberalism. We do not share the absolute faith in God of the one or the unrestricted confidence in humankind of the other. For such as us, a third way in Judaism is gradually being clarified. The commanding power we only associated with Orthodoxy is now being linked to the personal autonomy we once only identified with universalistic liberalism. Recovering our sense of God as the transcendent partner of an autonomous humankind creates a new sense of Jewish Covenant partnership for us and opens up to American Jews the possibility of a post-modern, non-Orthodox authentic Jewish existence.

# Some Personal Words

Though many crafts have been depersonalized, an author is still encouraged to make some personal remarks about his work. I should like to carry on this worthy tradition with a few comments about the intellectual trail that led me to this book and about some friends who have been instrumental in my writing it.

A decade ago, as I began to devote my professional life to Jewish theology, I defined our immediate task as breaking with the century-and-a-half-old practice of writing theologies apologetically—that is, from the vantage of one who sought to validate Judaism to skeptics. Rather, I felt that we ought first to try to clarify what Judaism meant to those who still believed in it. My articles and books were, therefore, a series of methodological searches, seeking a way of working toward this inner-directed goal.

I was happy enough with my progress to begin work on a systematic exposition of Jewish faith, but two things happened which redirected my energies.

The one was the increasing social upheaval in America. For years my colleagues and I had preached about the glories of Jewish ethics and the relevance of Judaism to modern life. Now our young people and our own self-respect demanded that we either make good on those claims or shut up. The challenge was complicated by the realistic acknowledgment that, as against the days when the social implications of Judaism seemed easily equated with political liberalism, there was now no simple, single road from Jewish belief to Jewish social responsibility. I tried to respond to this situation by founding *Sh'ma,* the bi-weekly journal of Jewish social ethics which I edit. In the three years of its existence it has at least demonstrated that, though we may not have many clear-cut answers, we can illuminate our alternatives through our disputatious, Talmudic dialogue.

About the same time, my deeply intuitive friend Jacob Behr-man began insisting that I ought to try to explain to American Jewry the transition through which it was passing. Jacob had his own vision of what was going on, and though we had many long and spirited discussions about it, I never could figure out what he wanted me to do. Yet in the process of arguing with him I came to understand what I felt I had to say, and this book is the result.

Though this work is not directed to theological colleagues, I should like to explain what I see as the technical foundation of this effort. In substance, this is an apologetic theology of the Jewish doctrine of Israel, the people of God's Covenant. In com-posing it I have consciously moved beyond the approach I speci-fied in Chapter 8 of *How Can A Jew Speak of Faith Today*? Here I have substituted an existentialist analysis, organized around Paul Tillich's concern with ultimacy, for the direct po-lemic called for in the previous book. Only, as against some con-temporary Protestant heralds of transcendence amidst the secu-lar, I have focused on the ground of our commitment to value and duty—which I take for granted exists in most Jews—rather than seeking signs of being's infinity at the borders of our finitude. I think the difference in focus is typical of the differing root concerns of the two faiths. Nonetheless, one might well argue that, despite my existentialist reversal of the relation of values to faith, I am ultimately derivative from the nineteenth-century Protestant theologian Albrecht Ritschl, thus demonstrating that Judaism has close kin in some varieties of Christian faith. This may be true. What I have done here, then, is to bypass the epistemological abyss by a phenomenological approach to the validity of faith. I have utilized an existentialist analysis of commitments to personal and social values to open up the individual to the transcendent foundation on which he almost certainly grounds them. Perhaps such an approach would also work with Christianity. But my concern in this book is to speak to Jews, and in their case, I believe this approach is the most effective one I know.

I am deeply grateful to Theodore Solotaroff, who read an earlier version of this book and made many insightful suggestions as to how I might go about improving it. Peter Schwed has been unfailingly cordial and helpful in the process of bringing this book to the public. In its various stages, parts of the manuscript were typed by Sylvia Seldin, Drucy Borowitz and Anita Sokoloff, for whose skill I am most thankful. The final draft was put into proper form by Lillian Morgan of the HUC-JIR secretarial staff, and I cannot praise her diligence and intelligence too highly.

And now that the several years of work on this manuscript end in its publication, I express again, and again inadequately, my gratitude to God, who in His goodness, has enabled me to reach this hour:

אַשְׁרֵינוּ. מַה־טּוֹב חֶלְקֵנוּ. וּמַה־נָּעִים גּוֹרָלֵנוּ. וּמַה־יָּפָה יְרֻשָּׁתֵנוּ. אַשְׁרֵינוּ שֶׁאֲנַחְנוּ
מַשְׁכִּימִים וּמַעֲרִיבִים עֶרֶב וָבֹקֶר . וְאוֹמְרִים פַּעֲמַיִם בְּכָל־יוֹם.

שְׁמַע יִשְׂרָאֵל . יְיָ אֱלֹהֵינוּ . יְיָ אֶחָד:

"Happy are we! How good is our portion, how pleasant our lot, how beautiful our heritage, that morning and evening, twice each day, we say 'Hear, O Israel, Adonai our God, Adonai is one.'"

EUGENE B. BOROWITZ

Hebrew Union College-
Jewish Institute of Religion
The New York School